# The Invention of Dolores del Río

*Chioma Ugochukwu*

# The Invention of Dolores del Río

Joanne Hershfield

University of Minnesota Press

Minneapolis

London

A significantly different version of chapter 2 originally appeared as "Race and Romance in *Bird of Paradise*," *Cinema Journal* 37, no. 3 (spring 1998): 3–15.

Published by the University of Minnesota Press
111 Third Avenue South, Suite 290
Minneapolis, MN 55401-2520
http://www.upress.umn.edu

Library of Congress Cataloging-in-Publication Data

Hershfield, Joanne, 1950–
    The invention of Dolores del Rio / Joanne Hershfield.
       p.    cm.
    Includes index.
    ISBN 0-8166-3409-2 (alk. paper) — ISBN 0-8166-3410-6 (pbk. : alk. paper)
       1. Del Rio, Dolores, 1905–   2. Motion picture actors and actresses—
    Mexico—Biography.   3. Minorities in the motion picture industry—United
    States.   I. Title.
       PN2318.D4 H47 2000
       791.43'028'092—dc21

                                                        99-050768

Printed in the United States of America on acid-free paper

The University of Minnesota is an equal-opportunity educator and employer.


11  10  09  08  07  06  05  04  03  02  01  00        10  9  8  7  6  5  4  3  2  1

# Contents

# Acknowledgments

I am grateful to family, friends, and colleagues whose advice and encouragement have sustained me through the long process of completing this book. They are too numerous to mention, but I would like to offer thanks to a few whose minds and shoulders were always available.

The women in my writing group—Jan Bardsley, Altha Cravey, and Megan Matchinske—have provided critical insight, chocolate, and wine for more than two years. Ultimately, they helped make the book eminently more readable. Ken Hillis, Hap Kindem, Victoria Johnson, Anna McCarthy, Zuzanna Pick, Patricia Torres San Martín, Britta Sjogren, and Ann Marie Stock offered reassurance and words of wisdom.

Bill Balthrop, chair of the Department of Communication Studies at the University of North Carolina at Chapel Hill, authorized research leaves, and the University Research Council provided continuing support. The Institute of Arts and Humanities, under the direction of Ruel Tyson, granted me a fellowship that provided a semester off from teaching. My fellow "fellows" in the institute helped me to shape the manuscript.

The Duke-UNC Institute for Latin American Studies awarded me two travel grants that supported research and good food in Mexico. Mary Corliss and Terry Geeskin at the Film Stills Archive at the Museum of Modern Art gathered together stills from del Río's Hollywood films. David R. Maciel searched the vaults of Filmoteca and Cineteca Nacional in Mexico City for stills from del Río's Mexican films. Thanks also to Alejandro Pelayo for permission to reprint production stills from del Río's Mexican films. Various readers, including Daniel Bernardi and David Desser, helped shape earlier versions of some chapters. My editor at the University of Minnesota Press, Jennifer Moore, rescued the manuscript (and me) with her generous and timely support of the project. Her staff provided needed and valuable editorial assistance.

Finally, and always, everything is possible because of Jim and Gillian.

# Introduction

When *Photoplay* conducted a search in 1933 for the "most perfect feminine figure in Hollywood," using "medical men, artists, designers" as
judges, the "unanimous choice" of these selective arbitrators of female
beauty in the United States was the Mexican actress Dolores del Río.[1] The
question posed by the fan magazine's search and the methodology it employed to find "the most perfect feminine figure" reveal a number of parameters that defined femininity and female beauty during that particular
moment in U.S. history. At the same time, the selection of Dolores del Río
presents an enigma: Given the particular environment of social attitudes
and beliefs in the 1930s around questions of racialized sexuality, why is it
that a foreign star like del Río was considered more beautiful than such
popular white stars as Irene Dunne, Fay Wray, and Norma Shearer? In this
volume, I interrogate this enigma. In the following pages, I examine how
Hollywood engaged the body of a foreign female movie star, at various
moments and in different ways, to symbolize the nexus of gender and race.

This book is not a biography of María Dolores Asúnsolo López-
Negrete, born in the city of Durango, Mexico, on August 3, 1904. Instead, I
analyze the sexual and racial imaging of Dolores del Río, the movie star
fashioned in Hollywood, California, by an industry whose business it was

*María Dolores Asúnsolo López-Negrete. Photograph courtesy of the Museum of Modern Art, New York.*

to manufacture, promote, and distribute commodities.[2] Although del Río never became a cultural icon in the same way that Mae West, Greta Garbo, or Marilyn Monroe did, her presence in American popular culture over a period of fifty years offers a particularly rich case study of America's shifting imagination of racialized sexuality.[3]

Although I am using the case of a particular movie star to address the intersection of race and sex, I do not assume that Hollywood's version of race was unique.[4] The way in which a culture defines those who are "different" is regulated to a large extent by how that culture categorizes what it "sees." To understand how a movie star is read in our culture, therefore, we must understand the connotative power of the cinematic body as a *visual* sign figured within broad cultural notions of beauty and sexuality.

The movie star is arguably one of the more meaning-inflected signs in Hollywood movies. In addition to symbolizing obvious physical characteristics such as race and gender, the star's physiognomy, actions, clothes, and demeanor all contribute to the individualization of the film character by inferring emotional and moral traits. The star's body also denotes abstract concepts such as class, beauty, moral characteristics, and particular idiosyncratic qualities that mark a character as an individual. Yet this body is not a "real" individual in the sense of a social, material being but is rather a sign of a social phenomenon.[5] She is a sign of other signs: she may signal femaleness, youth, wealth, madness, sexual availability, virginity, whiteness, and/or foreignness. The readings of a star "sign" and her image are not open to any interpretation but are limited by a range of possible meanings.[6]

Rather than disguise or ignore the enigma of race, Hollywood often chose to capitalize on the economic possibilities of difference. For example, the popularity of the early cinema star Sessue Hayakawa was built upon the industry's ability to exploit contemporary racial stereotypes of "Orientals." Donald Kirihara argues that because stereotypes about Asians circulated in popular discourses about race and ethnicity, Hollywood found them "useful" in narratives that were explicitly "about prejudice, discrimination, miscegenation, and acculturation."[7] What Kirihara is proposing is that Hollywood was not ideologically innocent about the kinds of racial and ethnic portrayals perpetrated in the movies. At the same time, his observations suggest that producers and directors were very much compelled by the same sets of cultural knowledge that their audiences were. Those who participated in the production and consumption of Hollywood movies in the 1910s and 1920s understood precisely the functions of stereotypes and the meanings that those stereotypes generated. Audiences recognized Hayakawa as Japanese and perceived that the characters he portrayed in films were necessarily linked to certain "essential" traits that were ideologically conjoined to "Japaneseness" and "Orientalism."

## Race and the Star Text in U.S. Cinema

National identity in the United States has been informed by the imagining of racial differences. The development of a U.S. national identity was initially envisioned as white, Anglo-Saxon protestant, and male. If women were national subjects, they had no political rights. Nonwhites (both males and females), on the other hand, were not figured as subjects of the nation at all; they were "others."

There is no necessary correspondence between ideas of race and nation. Instead, symbolic differences between "ourselves" and others are incorporated into the discourse of national identity. These differences constitute a particular aspect of this identity that Etienne Balibar and Immanuel Wallerstein call "fictive ethnicity," an identification that has nothing to do with any kind of national "race" but only with our imagination of differences.[8] In the United States in the twentieth century, this imagining was given visual form through the body of the movie star.[9]

Race is very evident on the body of the star. Indeed, one could say that stars like del Río *embody* race. What does this mean, to "embody" race?[10] Whereas contemporary critical discussions about the meaning of race focus on questions of identity and subjectivity, popular conceptions of racial definitions and differences are understood through the body. In the case of racial or ethnically coded characters in motion pictures, the obvious marks of race—skin color and facial characteristics—are reinforced through a character's accent, through the character's actions and values, and through her place and function in a film's narrative. The character's racial identity is also, however, necessarily inflected by the racial identity of the movie star who inhabits the character's body.

A movie star has no "personal identity" (even though the person who inhabits a star's body may claim such an identity). In other words, she is a figure composed of a presence and a set of discourses that symbolize an *iconic* identity. Of course, this figure of a symbolic identity did not originate with the cinema, but it was redeployed by the cinematic apparatus in particular ways. In the 1890s, the emergence of cinema coincided with the increasing importance of the body in social and cultural discourse.[11] Theories of the body were concerned with such marks of difference as physical abnormality and sexual and racial difference. Initial experiments with cinema technology were, in fact, interested in documenting the body in order to provide visible evidence for these scientific discourses about sex and race.[12]

Coincidental with the increase of discourses about the body and the development of new technologies that visualized this body, woman as a historical subject emerged as a new kind of "cultural and social category ... of 'trouble,'" in the words of E. Ann Kaplan.[13] It is not that women "suddenly" became objects to be looked at. They became different kinds of objects whose gendered identity proposed different implications for those who looked at them. The female movie star was one of the most visible enunciations of this new way of thinking about sexual difference.

If Hollywood could easily cast gender within the binary trope of male/female, the representation of race in cinema proved far more complicated. Whereas race, like gender, is played out on the body of the star, the complexity of racist ideology in the United States and the undeniable visibility of an actor's skin color and facial characteristics complicate cinematic racial categories. Hollywood's images clarified popular American beliefs about nonwhite peoples, beliefs that emerged from scientific and philosophical discourses and from racist institutional practices such as black slavery and the indentured servitude to which Chinese, Japanese, and Mexicans were subjected at various moments in American history. These discourses and practices were in turn presented in popular and high culture, including novels and paintings. With the invention of cinematography and other forms of mass technologies of cultural representations, images of racialized sexuality were dispersed throughout a wider and more heterogeneous population.[14] What is distinctive about Hollywood films is that race was made corporeal in the body of the movie star.

Given the fact that feminine beauty in the United States has always been conceived as "white" beauty, and given that most Hollywood stars have been white, how can we account for the success of "foreign" women such as Dolores del Río, the Brazilian "bombshell" Carmen Miranda, and the "Mexican spitfire," Lupe Vélez? It could be argued that American celebrities can rise above the color line, that they are "colorless." Yet if we read popular responses to nonwhite stars of the classical Hollywood cinema such as del Río and Dorothy Dandridge and to contemporary celebrities such as Denzel Washington and Jennifer Lopez, it is undeniable that our shared understanding of these figures takes into account their racial and/or ethnic identities.[15]

I am interested in the role of stars as "cultural signs" and as sites of cultural politics. However, I want to understand not only the ideological determinants of movie stars' public and cinematic meanings but also the industrial, economic, and political conventions and pressures that produce and constrain what is seen in neighborhood movie houses. I will argue throughout this book that even though del Río was an "other" in terms of her place in U.S. culture, the Hollywood industry folded her into the fabric of contemporary conceptions of female beauty through its promotional machinery and its narrative strategies. Because of her celebrity status in the very visible arena of American cinema, del Río became an "acceptable"

*The image of exoticism. Photograph courtesy of the Museum of Modern Art, New York.*

other while Mexicans in general were relegated to a lower status on the lad-
der of U.S. racial hierarchy.[16]

Del Río's star text was distinguished by a historically situated image of
an exotic foreign woman who was attracted to (and attractive to) white
men. When del Río arrived in Hollywood, the movie star was differentiated primarily by his or her physical image. This image was promoted

through a range of symbolic and economic practices, which included the popular discourses of fan and trade magazines, the popular press, advertising, and the films in which the star appeared.[17] The intent of promotional campaigns was to familiarize the public with the product and to differentiate that product from other similar products.

Throughout this book, I examine popular media such as consumer publications, newsmagazines, and newspaper articles and editorials. These texts are situated in relation to scientific and popular discussions about national identity and race in the United States during particular historical moments. I analyze how stars function in general ideological and cultural terms and in public discourse, and, secondarily, how stars function within films themselves as responses to or contestations of those terms.

Like other celebrities, del Río was more than an image: she was a carefully constructed commodity that circulated cultural conceptions and values between producers and consumers of popular culture about beauty, feminine sexuality, national identity, and race. Although female stars are defined primarily along a scale of sexual desirability, the color of del Río's skin and her facial characteristics marked her first of all as not white.[18]

In the following chapters, I analyze how del Río's racialized image questioned standards of white femininity and how Hollywood positioned her as an object of white male desire within a continuing climate of cultural and legal injunctions against miscegenation. Given Hollywood's obsession with heterosexual romance and its narrative promotion of monogamy, the enigma of cinematic interracial romance needs to be interrogated. The presence of racially coded actresses like del Río on Hollywood's screens provoked a complex anxiety in American audiences. This anxiety cannot be reduced to either race or gender but must be examined within the constellation of racialized sexuality bound up with the notion of national identity.

Del Río's career in Hollywood spans more than fifty years, a time frame that allows for a diachronic examination of the transformation of stories about race and gender in the United States. The "meaning" of del Río at particular historical moments was a "set of meanings" that cannot be read merely as a function of contextual or extratextual factors; the connotation and denotation of del Río's body varied from film to film. Her gender, the articulation of her sexuality, and the meaning of her nonwhite body were clarified through each film's narrative and mise-en-scène and through the context of reception.[19] In turn, the films recirculated ideas of racialized sexuality back into culture.

Throughout this volume I ask the following questions in relation to the meanings del Río's body offered up to her audience: What was cinema's place in defining sexuality and race? Why did producers and directors choose particular representations of racialized gender? Where did these representations come from? Answering these questions requires consideration of the complex interactions among numerous social texts and cultural practices around problems of race and sexuality.

# 1

## Inventing Dolores del Río

*She was rich. She was happily married. She had everything she wanted. Dolores Del Rio came to Hollywood seeking neither fame nor romance nor money. She went into the movies "just for fun." But the movies refuse to let her go, because she is one of the great discoveries of the year.*

Ivan St. Johns, "A Daughter of the Dons," *Photoplay*, June 1927

Dolores del Río was twenty years old when she was "discovered" in Mexico by Hollywood producer and director Edwin Carewe. At Carewe's urging, del Río came to Hollywood in 1925 with her husband, Jaime. The del Ríos were part of a diverse and massive wave of Mexican immigration to the United States between 1910 and 1930. This exodus from Mexico was motivated by the social and economic turbulence of the Mexican Revolution, encouraged by the absence of U.S. immigration quotas on Latin American immigrants and fueled by the demand for low-wage workers in agriculture in the southwestern region of the United States.

Although the majority of these immigrants initially came to the United States to do farmwork, by the 1930s most of them had moved into urban areas of the Southwest.[1] Between 1910 and 1930 almost 10 percent of Mexico's population emigrated to the United States. In 1924, the U.S. Congress implemented an immigration quota in the form of the Sherman Act. Quotas based on national origin according to the 1890 census were enacted, "limiting the admissible number of any nationality to 3 per cent of the foreign-born members of that nationality residing here."[2] The politicians were concerned primarily with regulating immigrants from eastern and southern Europe. Mexican workers were welcomed because of the

*The invention of Dolores del Río. Photograph courtesy of the Museum of Modern Art, New York.*

agricultural and technical competence they brought to a rapidly expanding market for those kinds of skills.

In Los Angeles, despite discrimination and racial stereotyping, many Mexicans found work in the film industry as technicians, cinematographers, directors, and actors.[3] Lupita Tovar, Lupe Vélez, Delia Magaña, Gilbert Roland, and Ramón Novarro (del Río's cousin), to name a few successful Mexican immigrants, were even able to rise to stardom, although their roles were limited by trenchant racial ideologies.

During the early years of American cinema, white actors played racial, ethnic, and "half-breed characters"; Asian actors played American Indians and Mexicans; and Mexicans portrayed half-breed Indians and Polynesian princesses. However, as a rule, whereas both white actors and ethnic actors could portray ethnic and racial others, Mexican and other actors coded "nonwhite" never played "white" characters or assumed the same kinds of roles as designated "white" actors.[4]

This cinematic practice of "racial cross-dressing" contributed to the production of America's "national culture." According to Michael Rogin, during a period of mass immigration of Irish and Jewish refugees, Hollywood movies took part in "making visible the significance of race in the continuing creation of American [racial] identity," a significance that had been sublimated by the turn of the century.[5] Racial cross-dressing, or "masquerade," in movies and other forms of popular culture revealed the extent to which America's creation of its national identity was founded in an understanding of racial inequality and ethnic descent. Cinematic racial and ethnic masquerade "acknowledged the ambiguous racial status" white ethnics occupied, while at the same time "demonstrated the European's difference from" nonwhite racial and ethnic groups.[6] Skin color thus became a primary marker of American national identity.

The equation between color of skin and racial designation inflected the ways in which Mexican actors were labeled. Light-skinned Latino/as were more easily able to move in and out of ethnic roles.[7] For example, Gaylyn Studlar examines how Antonio Moreno, a light-skinned Mexican, was "promoted" to whiteness in the late 1910s so that by the following decade he was both "the right kind of ethnic" and "thoroughly Anglicized."[8] Additionally, the label of *Spanish* removed certain actors from the more negative connotation of *Mexican*. Others, with darker skins, were stuck with the stereotypical "greaser, bandido, and 'Native' roles."[9] "Spanish" characters were generally landowning, aristocratic, well-educated, and graced with acceptable social skills. "Mexicans" were poor, violent, uneducated, and unrefined. As a consequence, many Latino/a actors were advised to change their names and hide their ethnic identities, if possible, if they wanted to get ahead in Hollywood.[10]

Paradoxically, the studios used the "Mexican" ancestry of a few successful stars, such as Ramón Novarro, Lupe Vélez, and del Río, to market them. In these instances, Hollywood exploited the success of its commodities, relying on the public's fascination with and desire for exoticism. At the same

*Del Río as the "perfect Latin type." Here she is played against the "white" actress Claire Windsor. Photograph courtesy of the Museum of Modern Art, New York.*

time, the industry realized the need to differentiate among its foreign recruits. Just as Garbo was dubbed the "Nordic beauty," del Río "a daughter of the Dons," became "the perfect Latin type," while Lupe Vélez was most definitely Mexican: "black-haired, black-eyed, slender, small, and untamed."[11]

Carewe gave del Río a small role as a vamp named Carlotta de Silva in *Joanna* (1925). After a few bit parts, her first leading role was in First National's *Pals First* (1926) opposite Lloyd Hughes. That same year she was selected as one of the "WAMPAS Baby Stars" in an annual beauty pageant put on by the Western Association of Motion Picture Advertisers that promoted young actresses headed for stardom. The 1926 lineup also included future stars Mary Astor, Fay Wray, Joan Crawford, and Janet Gaynor.

A subsequent starring role in Raoul Walsh's *What Price Glory* (1926), as Charmaine, a French barmaid, solidified del Río's status as a certified "movie star."[12] She was in demand after Walsh's picture and appeared in an adaptation of Leo Tolstoy's *Resurrection,* directed by Carewe, in 1927; she then appeared in *The Loves of Carmen* (1927, Walsh), *The Trail of '98* (1928, Clarence Brown), and *Ramona* (1928, Carewe), the third film version of Helen Hunt Jackson's popular nineteenth-century novel.

Many of del Río's 1920s films do not survive, and only one or two reels of others still exist. Some films have left no celluloid traces and are available to us only through extant promotional materials or written critical and popular discourse. For example, a promotional advertisement in the May 21, 1927, issue of *Exhibitors Herald* announces the screening of two films starring del Río, *Jungle Rose* ("a tropical tempest of emotion on the Amazon" and "a daring, exotic romance of London and the Jungle") and *In My Wife's Honor.* I have not been able to find any other reference to either of these two films. How then can these hypothetical texts be analyzed? How can it be determined what the films, and del Río, might have meant to Hollywood and to her various audiences? If, as Tom Gunning argues, "rigorous textual analysis is vital to the social history of film" (an argument with which I agree), how then can the absent text contribute to an understanding of its meaning in its particular social context?[13]

Giuliana Bruno faced the same dilemma in her investigation of the silent films of Italian filmmaker Elvira Notari. Bruno's solution was to analyze a text's "fictional referents," what she defines as the "margins" of a text. Through a process of what she calls "streetwalking on a ruined map,"

*Del Río achieves star status as Charmaine in Raoul Walsh's* What Price Glory. *Photograph courtesy of the Museum of Modern Art, New York.*

Bruno retraces the remnants of Notari's absent films—film reviews, promotions, and advertising—as well as public discourse about Notari and her work. The purpose of this kind of analytic "streetwalking" is not to reconstruct the intrinsic meaning of a text, but to fashion an understanding about what the films *could* have meant to Notari's audiences or, at least, to bring to light possible meanings.[14] I would argue for the use of the same tactics in reconstructing the meaning of a star text. As Studlar puts it, in order to understand the production and consumption of Hollywood stars, scholars must "go beyond these film texts to the extratextual materials that were used to create stardom for the public's consumption [and farther] to the broader historical field of American culture."[15]

Given the absence of many of del Río's early films, I am forced to wander among textual and contextual encrustations of these missing texts. In this chapter I examine scripts, movie reviews, trade and fan magazine editorials and letters, production papers, and studio exhibition and distribution promotion and advertising materials, as well as censorship files from a number of del Río's films from the 1920s.

At the same time, an interpretation of readings based on considerations of difference is, at best, an informed "fabrication" of history, in the words of Michel de Certeau.[16] The fabrication of film histories is first of all limited by disciplinary and institutional conventions. The institutions of cinema and film scholarship work to preserve the material and ideological culture of film in what Janet Staiger terms "less than neutral ways."[17] That is to say, much of the historical material that is available for us to examine has been conserved in accordance with certain institutional and ideological tactics. For example, only *certain* films, fan magazines, and press clippings of *particular* films and movie stars are archived in libraries. Nonetheless, Staiger believes that through a dialectical process of moving back and forth between evidence and theory it is possible to develop a "historical 'explanation' of the event of interpreting a text," of determining what a film or a movie star like del Río could have meant to patrons of the neighborhood cinema houses of the 1920s.[18]

## Mapping the 1920s

Although the 1920s cannot be separated out from the preceding decade, which was defined by the war in Europe, and the subsequent decade of the Depression, there are a number of "distinctive qualities" that mark that period in U.S. history. Lynn Dumenil names these qualities as "unprecedented prosperity . . . a period of conservatism in which politicians and pundits alike celebrated Big Business as the savior of American democracy and enterprise," the reputation of the roaring twenties—"of a fast life, propelled by riches and rapidly changing social values," nativism and the escalation of racial and ethnic tensions between white, Anglo-Saxon Protestant Americans and African Americans, Catholics, Jews, and other immigrants. The twenties were also marked by isolationism, urbanization, "changing values and behavior in sexual, religious, and other private realms," and the explosion of mass-culture production and venues.[19]

One of the more potent images of this period is that of the "new woman." In 1920, (white) women acquired the right to vote in the United States. The (white) woman was now seen as a citizen. She was described as independent, as a sexually desirable and desiring subject. However, she also signified for a large majority of the population the negative aspects of modernity. Significantly, it was the emerging quality of feminine desire that seemed to threaten existing ideologies of the nuclear family, American masculinity, and white superiority.

Although symptoms of this "new American woman" were first seen at the turn of the century, Dumenil argues that her central place in the public's imagination did not take hold until the 1920s.[20] During the "jazz age," skirts moved up above the knee and hair was bobbed; society girls and salesclerks alike traded in woolen tights for silk stockings, and respectable young middle-class women found jobs outside of the home and smoked and drank in public. The modern mass-market cosmetics industry actively promoted the "made-up woman" as an ideal to which all women should aspire.[21]

The new woman was envisioned as the principal consumer in an era that embraced "the emergence of America as a consumer culture." Not only was there more money and more products available for the working and middle classes, there was a transformation in individual values from an ethics that revered "restraint and order" into one that embraced "leisure, consumption, and self-expression as vehicles for individual satisfaction." Corporate culture promoted consumption as necessary for "progress" and the economic development of American society, and American workers perceived the "freedom" to buy as an "antidote to the loss of power in the modern world."[22]

Urbanization and the corresponding shift in urban work schedules provided workers with extended moments of leisure—an eight- or nine-hour workday that left evenings and weekends free and provided many with paid summer vacations. Leisure and recreation were commercialized in the form of an explosion of public entertainments available for reasonable prices, including amusement parks, nightclubs, sporting events, recorded popular music, and more (and more fabulous) movie theaters. Although white-collar and blue-collar workers participated in these entertainments to varying degrees, Americans of all classes and races spent a lot of their expendable income and time at their neighborhood cinemas.

Hollywood movies sold more than leisure, however. The men and women and the lifestyles portrayed in the movies were significant marketing vehicles for the products necessary for a life of repose. Although audiences did not passively incorporate the messages that Hollywood purveyed, people made choices and exercised preferences that were limited by the range of possibilities, choices that, in turn, were fed back into the system of production and consumption.[23]

One of the jobs of the female movie star was to recruit members of her female audience—primarily young, middle-class women who had money to spend—to the role of consumer. Thus, at the same time stars were commodities in themselves, they were also engaged in the business of selling material and ideological products, beauty merchandise and clothes as well as ideologies of female beauty. Actresses such as Dorothy Mackaill and Constance Bennett modeled dresses they had worn in their recent films, dresses that were available for purchase through *Photoplay*'s "Shopping Service."[24] Beautiful female stars portrayed women who attracted men through their looks and their clothes and were emulated by avid consumers of movies and fan magazines. Advertising discourse about beauty in magazines such as *M'Lady Beautiful, Ladies' Home Journal, McClure's, Women's World*, and *Good Housekeeping* amplified the industry's focus on female beauty as a commodity to be exploited.[25] And women responded to and embraced this major marketing effort with enthusiasm. Cosmetic sales soared from $17 million to more than $140 million by the middle of the decade.[26]

By the 1920s, Hollywood's stars were setting the fashion for style and beauty through the marketing of the stars themselves and through product tie-ins. "A cult of youthfulness, sensuality, and beauty" defined femininity in the 1920s and "made millionaires out of Coco Chanel, Charles Revson, Helena Rubinstein, and Elizabeth Arden."[27] The leading fan magazine, *Photoplay*, ran a regular feature, "How to Dress for Trying Roles," that advised women on what to wear (and not wear) for the daily "roles" of real life, including gardening, tennis, and washing dishes.[28] Other daily roles were ignored, however. As Peiss has shown, the beauty industry "abjured depicting women in the public realm traditionally occupied by men—the workplace, meeting hall, and polling booth."[29]

Manufacturers of products such as Pond's cold cream, Ivory soap, and

Listerine mouthwash recruited stars to advertise their products, selling "beauty" as well as products. *Photoplay* published an "advice" column that debated popular questions about female roles, such as the value of virginity, the development of the "perfect" figure, the advisability of becoming a stage star, and the issue of working wives.

Although the "most beautiful women" were young and white, and Clara Bow, Hollywood's "It Girl," was America's national sweetheart, the arrival from other countries of a number of "exotic" movie stars such as Pola Negri, Greta Garbo, and del Río advanced a different kind of female beauty, one that intruded upon changing American ideals of national and gendered identities.[30] Del Río's position in American popular culture challenged (but did not entirely displace) negative stereotypes about foreigners in general and Mexicans in particular. In an era of racist nativism, she was a foreigner who was celebrated as one of the most beautiful women in the United States. In fact, it was precisely this foreignness that defined her attraction: Hollywood repeatedly situated del Río as a foreign, exotic woman in films about exotic locations, and she consistently responded to her audience's understanding of what and who an "exotic" woman was.[31]

Fatimah Tobing Rony rightly argues that "the exotic is always known."[32] At the same time, we recognize the meaning of the "exotic" in opposition to that which is known. The "exotic" has no absolute meaning outside of the sociohistorical context in which it is employed. *Exoticism* and *foreignness* are ambiguous terms that function ahistorically. There is no necessary link between the sign of "exoticism" and its situated referent as something that is alien, unusual, wondrous, or malevolent. The link is ideological but is inflected by the semiotic circumstance of an utterance and its reception. Thus del Río's exoticism and foreignness could function as elements to be admired, even sought after through sexual desire, fashion, and makeup. In the 1920s, exoticism became a style, a cult figure that was sought after and emulated. Peiss points to products such as "Stein's Mexicola Rouge and Hess's Indianola Paste." She quotes an Armand advertisement that advised, "A dark skin may be your greatest attraction—you may be hiding it with a light powder."[33]

## Inventing del Río

Carewe worked with Henry Wilson, one of the best publicists in Hollywood, to market the image of a foreign, exotic Dolores del Río to the public.[34] Wilson launched a campaign to keep the new star in the public eye by providing a continuous supply of stories and photos to trade and fan magazines. This early publicity presented the young Mexican star as "glamorous" and "aristocratic" by emphasizing her highborn status, her convent education, and her European training in ballet and art.[35]

In addition to being "exotic" and "aristocratic," del Río was feminine. Her positioning as a "feminine" woman who preferred long hair and a stylish, classic wardrobe to the bobbed hair, slim sheaths, and short hems of the flapper set her apart and above the "average" American beauty. Del Río's class status also shaped her image. Hollywood repeatedly emphasized that she came from a very wealthy "ancient" Mexican family of "Spanish blood" and spoke five languages. In a 1928 book about del Río that was one of a series titled Thumb Prints of the Famous, Margery Wilson reveals the contemporary eugenic basis underlying standards of beauty and status while at the same time defining del Río's public persona:

> There is not a feature nor a line in all of Del Rio's physical and mental make-up suggestive of the peasant. . . . Every line and curve of her slender, lithe, beautifully proportioned, dainty body and queenly little head is the perfect essence of many generations of aristocratic breeding. The fiery pride of high-caste Castellan ancestors is in the quiver of her delicate nostrils.[36]

Ultimately, athough she often played the cinematic role of a lower-class "bad woman," del Río's public persona was that of a high-class ethnic woman of impeccable morals. This personal and private identity was carefully crafted by Carewe, by Wilson, by the studios that produced her films, and by del Río herself. Her real-life transgressions (her husband, from whom she was separated, died in Europe in the midst of rumors that she was having an affair with Carewe) seemed to have little effect on this persona.[37]

That del Río was concerned with the crafting of her public persona is revealed in letters she wrote to Carewe and to studio executives. In a letter to Carewe about the possibility of her starring in the title role of The Loves of Carmen, del Río admits that she likes the script "but it seems to me there are possibilities of including scenes of a lewd and vulgar nature." After viewing the completed film, she complained to a Mr. Sheehan at Fox that "there are two or three shots . . . where my limbs are exposed in a manner that is most embarrassing to me." She wanted these shots eliminated from the picture. She was also worried about appearing in a certain film titled Upstream because she believed "there are some risque scenes in it."[38] Despite her concerns, the studio marketed to the public's prurient interests by promoting Carmen as "a gripping story of a woman's passion, elemental, all-conquering."[39]

Del Río's ethnic and racial characteristics were foregrounded as the

*A "classic" beauty. Photograph courtesy of the Museum of Modern Art, New York.*

basis of her sexual appeal when she was described in *Photoplay* as "the raven-haired, olive-skinned sinuous-limbed Carmen." When *Photoplay* listed her in its monthly register of "best performances" (even though the magazine's reviewer panned the film), a poem, described as "a sonnet Impression of a Shadow Stage Best Performance" was composed in her honor by an anonymous *Photoplay* writer. The poem ends with this description: "Bright as a sunset coming after rain, / With hint of storms to follow—*you are Spain!*"[40] Fox announced in the *Exhibitors Herald* that the title role in Walsh's film "will be in the capable hands of Dolores del Río whose nationality and temperament are similar to the vivicious *[sic]* character of Carmen."[41]

It is hard to know whether del Río's anxiety was simply moral or motivated by professional concerns regarding the continued success of her films and her star status. If professional, her concerns were legitimate given the pressures placed upon stars by their studios. In 1922 the film industry organized an official and defensive response to local and national interference by forming a trade organization, the Motion Picture Producers and Distributors of America (MPPDA), and installing Will Hays as the organization's first president. Threatened by public outcries against the "immoral" content of much of its product and concurrent demands for governmental censorship, Hollywood turned to the MPPDA for advice on circumventing these external pressures. Hays put into place a list of "Don'ts and Be Carefuls," which was adopted by the film industry at its annual trade conference in 1927. The list enumerated certain acts and words that "shall not appear in pictures produced by members of this association, irrespective of the manner in which they are treated."[42] Aware of the way in which the public conflated actors' screen images with their private ones, the studios began to exercise more control over their stars.

Even before Hollywood stepped up its attention to the private lives of its prime assets, Carewe kept careful watch over del Río and her career. In various letters to Fox producer Sol Wurtzel, Carewe reminded Wurtzel that the star "is subject to my direction in all manners concerning script, representation, and costuming" and that "Miss del Río shall only be engaged in the production of high-class pictures and that under no circumstances shall she be required to do an act which is obscene or lewd or which might reflect upon her reputation, character, and religious and social standing."[43]

Despite del Río's and Carewe's concern, however, *The Loves of Carmen* elicited a profusion of criticism for its presentation of female sexuality, criticism that revealed the extent to which a female movie star was identified with her onscreen persona. A letter from Jason S. Joy, director of the MPPDA's Department of Public Relations, to Fox executive Carl E. Milliken notes that "the picture is more of a study of Dolores del Rio's anatomy than anything else. . . . There are two sequences involving Dolores del Rio's drawers. . . . Jose is seen washing Del Rio's clothes." A friend wrote to Carewe that "experts with whom I have discussed the matter unequivocally predict that another such salacious production would irretrievable *[sic]* injure Miss Del Rio in motion pictures."[44] This "official" concern with her films, however, did little to detract from del Río's box-office appeal as a sexually provocative beauty. Shortly after the release of the film, *Photoplay* published its first feature about the Mexican star, calling her "one of the great discoveries of the year."[45] A month later, the fan magazine called her "the present leader of the Latin invasion" and insisted that "her sudden success has been equalled only by the Scandinavian Greta Garbo and the American Clara Bow."[46]

## Ramona

As I noted earlier, del Río rarely played a Mexican woman in her early career. The initial decades of silent cinema did create a number of female roles coded as "hispanic, including the cantina girl, the self-sacrificing Señorita, or the Vamp," whose function was to serve as "foils to or sex objects of Anglos" with much interracial heterosexual behavior.[47] These roles, however, were rarely played by Latina actresses.

Although del Río portrayed a Mexican in only a few of her films, the question of her "Mexicanness" figured prominently in the public discourse about her. Film reviewers often remarked upon her "Latin looks." In a review of *Pals First,* in which del Río plays a Louisiana heiress, a *Variety* reviewer criticized the casting, stating that del Río's "Latin type for one thing does not jibe with the aristocratic southern atmosphere, in addition to which Miss del Rio's personal accomplishments as a screen actress are negative." This remark reveals a particular understanding of a necessary relation between race and class on the one hand and, on the other, between class and geography. The reviewer also displays predominant beliefs about the conclusiveness of racial characteristics, writing that del Río's eyes, "of Oriental type, are an odd combination with the Spanish features."[48]

In one of her first starring roles for Carewe, del Río plays the title role in *Ramona,* an adaptation of a very popular 1884 novel by Helen Hunt Jackson (1831–85). The novel and the film narrate the melodramatic tale of a young girl who lives with her aunt, Señora Moreno, and cousin Felipe (Roland Drew) on their *hacienda,* or large ranch, in California. The novel foregrounds race in an interesting way: Ramona is ostracized not because she is Mexican, but because she is the illegitimate child of a white father and an Indian mother.[49] Subsequent film versions transformed this mixed ancestry in equivocal ways that are related to contemporary discourses about history and about race.[50] In his analysis of D. W. Griffith's 1910 film, *Ramona: A Story of the White Man's Injustice to the Indian,* Chon Noriega notes, for example, that the characters' Mexicanness is converted into

*Del Río in the title role of* Ramona. *Photograph courtesy of the Museum of Modern Art, New York.*

"Spanish," a more acceptable ethnic category during that decade. "Spanish-ness" was linked to revisions in the historiography of California's settlement and its history as a Mexican territory. This historical revisionism altered California's Mexican heritage and placed it within a "mythical past" called "Spanish California."[51] Noriega argues that such a rewriting of history has much larger and more profound implications for questions of race and ethnicity.[52]

Although no viewable copy of Carewe's *Ramona* survives, a wealth of contextual and extratextual material is available that situates the film in relation to discourses about race and in relation to Hollywood's narrational practices. Numerous film reviews provide plot summaries and descriptions of particular scenes. From these we can conclude that, in Carewe's film, Ramona is the daughter of Señora Moreno's brother, a Mexican, who had married an Indian woman.[53] Her white blood is thus summarily eradicated. When Ramona threatens to repeat her father's "mistake" by agreeing to marry Alessandro (Warner Baxter), an Indian sheepherder, the aunt forbids Ramona to see him and the couple runs away. After the deaths of Alessandro and their baby, Ramona is found by Felipe wandering in the mountains, suffering from amnesia. He takes her home to his mother's ranch, where they marry and live happily ever after.[54]

Publicity material for *Ramona* and popular reviews often linked the star's nationality and ethnicity with her film role. However, this material disclosed an equivocal understanding of who del Río might be, an understanding that revealed popular misconceptions of "Mexicanness." A reviewer for *Photoplay,* for example, praised del Río's performance, commenting that "there could have been no more fitting person to impersonate the Indian-blooded Ramona than the Mexican Dolores del Río" (the reviewer also notes that Warner Baxter "is well-cast as the Indian").[55] This review conflates "Indianness" with "Mexicanness" by collapsing two broad categories of race. First, although many Mexicans have Indian blood, few define themselves as "Indian." And second, del Río came from a wealthy European family that had never intermarried with Mexico's Indian population.

Other promotional materials focus on del Rio's wealthy status, revealing that the star wears "old family jewels belonging to her grandmother . . . and pieces of silks and laces . . . hundreds of years old" and that the star "has built a Mexican home in Hollywood's hills that is an exact replica of her home in Mexico."[56] Two promotional photos in the *Exhibitors Herald* are diametrically opposed. One photo features del Río the flapper, wearing her hair tucked up inside a stylish cloth hat and sporting long strands of pearls. On the next page, her long hair hangs down in braids and a single silver Indian bracelet adorns her wrist.[57]

Despite the film's success, it elicited a number of internal memos that evidence the industry's concern with *Ramona*'s portrayal of Mexicans. During the early years of the decade, questions of international interest in the MPPDA were handled separately from domestic issues; however, after 1927, foreign matters were overseen by the same public relations division that dealt with problems in the home market.[58] The year before *Ramona* was released, a United Artists film called *The Dove* (1927, Roland West) provoked a strong response from Mexico because of its negative portrayal of Mexicans. Various Latin American nations and Spain signed treaties agreeing to ban U.S. films that portrayed Latin American nations and peoples in a derogatory manner.

Whereas Hollywood was attentive to overseas box-office revenues, the U.S. State Department was anxious about the projection of the United States on the screens of potential allies and trading partners as well as Hollywood's portrayals of other nations and their peoples.[59] A letter from Major F. L. Herron to Jason S. Joy, director of the MPPDA, emphasized national concern regarding "negative" portrayals of Mexicans in Hollywood films: "'Inspiration' [Carewe's production company], I understand, is making a picture of 'Ramona' which is a Mexican story throughout, as I remember, but you might check up on it to see that they don't get into the wrong path and in trouble with Mexico on this."[60]

Mexico was not one of the industry's largest markets, but it was a significant one, given that Hollywood films accounted for 90 percent of the total films screened in Mexico. Helen Delpar argues that in the 1920s the American film industry's concern with the responses of Latin American officials to Hollywood's films must "be seen in the context of the filmmakers' efforts to exploit new opportunities" in that region.[61]

Mexican officials had continually objected to the "greaser" stereotypes that pervaded Hollywood westerns from 1906 through the 1920s and finally resorted to banning all the films of offending production companies in 1922.[62] Although Hollywood did respond to this pressure by allowing Mexican officials to review scripts that made reference to Mexico and Mexicans, the Mexican government was still complaining about the same negative stereotypes in 1927. Delpar cites a 1927 letter from the secretary of the Mexican embassy that reiterated Mexico's policy of banning offensive films. Delpar also points out that Hollywood seemed to be aware of its obligations and exhibited "greater sensitivity to national feelings" as evidenced by the Production Code's affirmation that "the just rights, history, and feelings of any nation are entitled to consideration and respectful treatment . . . and shall be represented fairly."[63]

Throughout the 1920s, del Río continued to portray foreign and/or ethnic characters. In *Revenge* (1928), she plays a Gypsy. In another film with Carewe, an adaptation of Leo Tolstoy's *Resurrection* (1927), she is cast as a Russian peasant girl who becomes a prostitute after being abandoned by her lover, a Russian prince. *The Trail of '98* offers her a chance to portray an "American" ethnic. In this film about the California gold rush, she plays a young Jewish girl, the granddaughter of an old Jew searching for certain wealth. According to Hollywood, because she was a "foreigner," del Río was particularly well situated to play a role in Hollywood's representation of the melting-pot thesis.[64] In the 1930s, however, the cinematic melting pot was reconsidered with the introduction of the industry's Production Code, a set of "does and don'ts" that was to shape Hollywood's vision of race relations for three decades.

# 2

# Race and Romance

*Nevair, nevair, will I make a Talkie, I zink zey are tairibble.*

Dolores del Río, quoted in Parrish, *Anxious Decades*, 1992

In March 1928, a number of Hollywood's most popular stars gathered in Mary Pickford's United Artists bungalow. Pickford and her husband, Douglas Fairbanks, were joined by Charlie Chaplin, Norma Talmadge, Gloria Swanson, John Barrymore, D. W. Griffith, and Dolores del Río. The occasion was a national radio program, organized by United Artists president Joseph Schenck, that was "designed to prove to millions of fans that their idols had voices, 'speaking' voices, good enough to meet the challenge of the talkies."[1] Del Río, currently starring in the role of Ramona, sang the popular title song from that film in English.[2]

Irrespective of the scare stories, anxieties, and panic attacks that struck Hollywood over the question of sound in film, by the end of 1928 "no fewer than 300 talkie pictures had been scheduled for production."[3] As a number of critics have indicated, sound films "renewed as well as revised" the theretofore successful devices and strategies of silent films.[4] At the same time, sound revolutionized Hollywood in a number of significant and unexpected ways. Most notably, Hollywood films were now audibly American. According to Richard Maltby and Ian Craven, sound films allowed for a recognition of the "cultural diversity of the street, playing accent off against accent" of Irish-, Swedish-, and Italian-inflected English.[5]

However, the "Americanness" of sound films also marked out what was *not* American, or not American enough. In del Río's case, for example, her ambiguous Spanish accent-inflected voice underscored her visible appearance as a "foreigner."

Despite her accent and her insistence that she would "nevair make a talkie," del Río weathered the industry's shift to sound. Hollywood continued to use her foreignness to its own benefit by moving her in and out of a variety of roles as an exotic, foreign woman. Her first sound films included the melodramatic *Evangeline* (1929, Carewe); the musical *The Bad One* (1930, George Fitzmaurice), in which she plays a French prostitute; and *Madame DuBarry* (1934, William Dieterle), in which she starred as "a dazzling courtesan who toyed with a King of France."[6]

This chapter focuses on del Río's role as the "savage princess, Luana" in King Vidor's 1932 film *Bird of Paradise,* one of Hollywood's numerous ethnographic metaphors in which Western prohibitions against miscegenation are disguised as a story of romantic love thwarted by the laws of nature. Vidor's film tells the story of Johnny Baker (Joel McCrea), a young American who jumps ship on a South Sea island, falls in love with a brown-skinned princess, and "goes native." The *New York Herald Tribune* noted that del Río's performance "is perhaps no more skillful or experienced than usual, but her dusky, alien beauty fits in so effectively with her role."[7]

The *Tribune's* description of del Río's beauty as "alien" exposes certain culturally repressed notions at work in *Bird of Paradise,* in the United States, and in Hollywood film in the 1930s, notions located at the intersection of race and gender. Del Río's "dusky" beauty contrasts sharply with the "duskiness" of the other native women in the film, whose skin tones are much darker than hers and whose facial features and body types are not coded with the same ideals of Western beauty as del Río's are.[8] In fact, the only other female singled out in the film is older, darker, overweight, asexual, and identified as "unattractive" by Western standards.[9]

If del Río performed on one level like white, female movie stars as an object of the white hero's desire, she could not occupy exactly the *same* narrative and visual space as foreign "white" actresses of the thirties such as Greta Garbo and Marlene Dietrich. In *Shanghai Express* (1932, Josef von Sternberg), for example, Dietrich, as Shanghai Lily, intercedes between her ex-lover, the good white Englishman, Doc Harvey (Clive Brook) and the bad Eurasian, Chang. As a reward for her role in helping to restore power to the rightful male (the white one), she is honored with Harvey's love. Garbo's mission as a "white" ethnic woman in *Anna Christie* (1930,

Clarence Brown) is to bring together American white males of differing ethnic backgrounds—her father is Swedish and the man she loves is Irish—and to serve as the maternal vehicle for the reproduction of a new, but still white, American race. Her reward is their forgiveness and love and the opportunity to serve the two men and her country. Such narratives fit in with American's "progressive/liberal 'common sense' approach to race," which recognized that racial mixing was inevitable given the ethnic

The "whitening" of the nonwhite love object in Bird of Paradise. *Photograph courtesy of the Museum of Modern Art, New York.*

composition of the United States in the 1930s.[10] At the same time, there were implicit restrictions that defined the limits of this melting-pot theory and, as I have discussed in chapter 1, these restrictions were tied to skin color. The difference between del Río and a star like Dietrich is obvious: the German-born star is "white" according to racial classifications of the 1930s, whereas the Mexican-born star is not.

Dietrich always played designated white characters; del Río never did. In another of Dietrich's films with von Sternberg, *Blonde Venus* (1932), released the same year as *Bird of Paradise,* Dietrich portrays Helen Jones, a European-born immigrant married to an American, who becomes a prostitute in order to support her family. Although this narrative theme was common in the classical Hollywood film, a number of critics have commented on the obvious intersection of race and sexuality in *Blonde Venus,* a link that is not so prevalent in other films of that genre. This link is most evident in the "Hot Voodoo" musical number, in which Dietrich emerges from the costume of a black gorilla in a kind of striptease performance. What is being revealed in the striptease is, specifically, Helen's whiteness. Mary Ann Doane, for example, remarks that "it is as though white femininity were forcefully disengaged from blackness once and for all in the process of commodification of the image of white female sexuality. . . . Blackness functions here not so much as a term of comparison . . . but as an erotic accessory to whiteness."[11] E. Ann Kaplan also comments on the detachment of white sexuality from blackness. According to Kaplan, Helen is positioned as the object of white male desire while at the same time "colluding in the oppression of both black women and black men."[12] Helen's ethnicity, German, is whitened in relation to the black gorilla and to the chorus of women in blackface who perform race in the background. Read in the context of racialized sexuality in the 1930s, the white prostitute's forced alienation from race is significant in relation to the economics of white female sexuality, an economics that is invisible but central to the narrative of *Bird of Paradise.*

## Hollywood and the Education of Desire

In the 1930s, the United States experienced not only an economic crisis but a crisis of social and cultural values, as jobs, families, and social institutions were devastated.[13] The 1929 stock market crash exacerbated fears and concerns that had been building since the end of the nineteenth century, as the United States began changing from a predominantly white, rural, and Protestant nation to one marked by increased industrialization and urbanization, immigration and resulting ethnic friction, the migration of many African Americans from the South to cities in the Northeast in search of jobs, and the rise of a society consumed by commercial mass culture.

During this period, gender roles were again challenged and revised. After the wild excesses of the 1920s, American society moved to reclaim traditional ideals of femininity and women's roles in the home and in the public sphere. Hollywood took part in this transformation of ideals. The figure of the flapper (the name given to young, middle-class women fond of fashion, music, smoking, and parties and immortalized in the novels of F. Scott Fitzgerald) gave way to the feminine ideal of "natural beauty" in films and film promotion.

In 1933, *Photoplay* informed its readers that Hollywood now wanted natural "girls who radiated vitality, stamina, sincerity, the clean-cut, clear-eyed girls of this new era who typify the backbone of our nation and who emulate the sturdiness of our pioneer women." Playing off of President Roosevelt's New Deal programs and his National Relief Administration (NRA), and making references to the Production Code Administration, *Photoplay* noted:

> There's to be a new deal now in the way of girls, along with other codes which have come to mean so much in industry. The "NRA" functioning to pull America out of the rut has swung its force in the direction of femininity. . . . We've had enough of sirens and flappers and we're ready now for the sedative qualities of sobriety.[14]

According to *Photoplay,* Hollywood would do its part to support this new deal by ensuring that the "new" screen star would manifest those necessary qualities. She would be "sparkling with energy and as buoyantly peppy as we see Lyda Roberts to be. . . . Vitality and the unsophisticated beauty of carefree youth make Jean Parker irresistible. . . . gone are the days of languorous eyes and exotic make-up! The demand is for natural, healthy beauty like Betty Furness." "An American girl despite her foreign name," June Vlasek is "refreshingly vigorous. Her allure is the result of healthful activity, rigorously pursued."[15]

"Natural beauty" is an ambiguous term. On one hand, the emerging beauty industry purported to be able to sell women products that would make them beautiful. On the other hand, "natural beauty" seemed to be something certain women were born with. An article in *Photoplay* displays a picture of woman wearing a strange, masklike contraption over her head and face as three men in white coats study the contraption and take notes. The caption reads:

This strange invention by Perc and Ern Westmore and Max Factor measures your beauty to a thousandth of an inch. According to the inventors,
the nose should be same length as forehead and equal the distance between base of nose and tip of chin. Space between eyes should be width
of the eye. Mouth corners should not extend beyond eye pupils.[16]

The industry promoted the "languorous and seductive" del Río as "a
natural beauty": "Her raven hair has never known curling-iron or finger
wave," a columnist in *Photoplay* announces. The writer goes on to declare
that the actress wears her hair "in the straight, severe lines typical of the
high-class Spanish Senorita. It has never been cut. Her eyebrows are natural too. She plucks only a few stray ones near the eyelid. . . . She uses neither
powder nor rouge on the screen or off."[17]

Baron George Hoyningen-Huené, a French photographer, praises the
"natural" beauty of del Río in another *Photoplay* article, using numerous
metaphors of naturalness: "She wears less make-up than any of the other
stars I have met. . . . Her skin is like ripe fruit. . . . She requires no artifice
whatever—the supreme test."[18]

At same time, Hollywood and the beauty industry used this "natural
beauty" to sell movies, makeup, and clothing. Del Río often complained of
the peasant-style clothes she had to wear in her films. In product promotions, however, she was photographed wearing the latest fashions.[19] Despite the article that insisted del Río "requires no artifice whatever," she was
habitually featured in advertisements that promoted "beauty tricks of the
month." "Hollywood's Beauty Shop" relates that her "brows are slightly
emphasized with a black pencil. The pencil, smudged to softness, darkens
upper lid slightly above lash-line."[20]

In another article, del Río is pictured relaxing between filming scenes
for *Flying Down to Rio*. We are told that she "dusts powder from lashes and
brows with a small, thin brush." Readers are urged to "give beauty" in the
form of these brushes, "gay lipsticks," a "manicure kit gift," or "a powder
that brings forth all the natural beauty of her skin." Sylvia, "beauty adviser
to famous stage and screen stars," tells us, "You, too, can have the Beauty
Secret I gave Dolores del Rio"—a box of Ry-Krisp wafers along with a
"Personal Consultation Chart" and a "32-page booklet which contains the
same diets and exercises I used on the movie stars."[21]

Such a collapsing of seemingly opposite signifiers of beauty—exoticism
and naturalness—preserved del Río's star status in Hollywood through the
social and cultural turmoil of the 1930s. After the release of *Bird of Paradise,*
the industry reminded its audiences who del Río "really was" by reconcil-
ing the image of the "savage princess" with a conflicting star text that de-

*Despite her exotic roles, del Río was promoted by Hollywood as a thoroughly modern woman. Photograph courtesy of the Museum of Modern Art, New York.*

nied this caption. Underneath a still of del Río in her hula skirt, *Photoplay* asked, "Would you believe that wild hula dancer, gone as native as a grass skirt, is smart Dolores Del Rio, one of the most sedate and ladylike social leaders of the film colony?"[22]

Although an ethnic foreign star could be put forward as one of the most beautiful woman in America, the question of intermarriage between a man and a woman of different races was not so easily promoted.[23] At the time *Bird of Paradise* was made, the portrayal of interracial affairs was not yet explicitly prohibited by the Production Code.[24] The film was in fact billed as a "flaming pageant of forbidden love . . . White man . . . brown girl."[25] A promotional poster featuring "Luana" wearing a grass skirt and bikini top in a seductive pose with a fire-breathing dragon behind her tells us that the fated couple is "caught in the torrid drama of life on a moon-drenched isle as the raging god in the Mountain sunders the earth, splits the skies and hurls the seas to a bottomless pit because they broke the savage taboo!"[26] The exotic land, the exotic religion, and the exotic woman are visually and, thus, narratively tied together as both erotic and destructive.

When the MPPDA eventually banned depictions of race mixing a few years later, the prohibition was clearly aimed at portrayals of affairs between "the white and the black races."[27] However, even if romantic entanglements between whites and other ethnic and racial groups were depicted, they were not officially sanctioned, and there were narrative limits imposed upon these depictions.[28]

In order to understand the logic behind Hollywood's unofficial policy, it is necessary to clarify the difference between two related but distinct terms: *interracial romance* is about desire and sex, whereas *miscegenation* is about bloodlines and procreation.[29] In the 1930s, Hollywood did not necessarily refuse to portray sexual relations between men and women of different races; it was reluctant, however, to depict racial interbreeding. Ramona Curry discusses the interracial affair between Mae West's character and a Chinese man in *Klondike Annie* (1936), noting, first of all, that "the Chinese man is played by a Caucasian actor" and, second, that the representation of the interracial affair serves to fetishize blonde, white female sexuality. In addition, Curry argues that West's public persona effaces Hollywood's representation of the "potential violation of interracial sexual taboos" in her films.[30] It is interesting that Hollywood and the viewing public expressed no obvious misgivings about del Río's affairs and marriages with white men. Perhaps her public persona as "one of Hollywood's most beautiful women" mitigated concerns about interracial sex.

In *Bird of Paradise*, sexual relations between the white American male and the brown-skinned princess are not censored. In fact, sex and sexuality are made visibly explicit in the film—the natives, Luana, and even Johnny wear little clothing; native dancing is presented as an orgiastic mating ritual; and finally, if sex between the American Johnny Baker and Luana is not directly depicted, it is explicitly implied.[31] What is prohibited in this film is miscegenation. This prohibition is couched in both narrative and representational terms: the story argues that racial mixing is "unnatural" in even the most primitive cultures, and the actress who portrays the Polynesian princess is "nonwhite" in the racial discourse of the United States in the 1930s.[32]

## Bird of Paradise, Miscegenation, and Tropes of Empire

Ella Shohat and Robert Stam link Vidor's film to a genre of exotic metaphors that, in their view, "played a crucial if contradictory role in constructing Eurocentric hierarchies."[33] An interest in the exotic permeated American cinema since its beginnings in the urban nickelodeons at the turn of the century.[34] Ethnographic documentaries and travelogues brought moving-picture visions of African, Asian, and South Seas cultures into the lives of white Western audiences. Fatimah Tobing Rony includes Hollywood cinema within the category of "ethnographic cinema," a cinema that relies on the fantasization and objectification of the racial body.[35]

Portrayals of race and ethnicity from other forms of popular culture, such as vaudeville and popular fiction, shaped cinematic racial portrayals. More significantly, the "epistemological guarantee" of cinematic representations served to verify Americans conceptions of racial and ethnic otherness. Race and racial stereotyping in film was (and is) immediately understood by audiences from New York City to Kansas City to Los Angeles. Skin, "the most visible of fetishes," is "the key signifier of cultural and racial difference in the stereotype," in the words of Homi K. Bhabha.[36] And Hollywood cinema has played a fundamental role in articulating racial stereotypes of exotic others.[37]

Although feminists have repeatedly pointed to Hollywood's positioning of women as commodities to be traded among men, in the case of colonial metaphors like *Bird of Paradise* (and in the Hollywood western, as I will show in chapter 4), the dark-skinned woman's function as an object of exchange is more complicated. These narratives often situate a white Western male against an other, non-Western, dark-skinned man. The "other" man, whose dark masculinity poses a sexual threat to the white man and Western imperialist patriarchy, is subsequently conquered through the appropriation of his woman. (The fact that the female other also embodies the threat of racial difference is initially ignored.)[38]

Kaplan remarks that in many of Hollywood's 1930s films about traveling, "male travellers envisage their journey through the sexual metaphor of mastering and conquering the female body . . . [which is also] a mastery of the primitive body, linked, as it were, to the female body."[39] According to Kaplan, the feminization of the exotic other is accomplished through a variety of strategies: infantilization, animalization, sexualization, and

Bird of Paradise *as ethnographic cinema. Photograph courtesy of the Museum of Modern Art, New York.*

debasement.[40] *Bird of Paradise* engages in each of these tactics and thus offers up an explicit example of the colonial metaphor of conquest.

The opening of *Bird of Paradise* sets the scene for an erotic encounter with an "other." As the yacht approaches the island, the local natives send a welcoming party of scantily clad men and women. In a bit of pseudo-ethnographic spectacle, the islanders engage in various diving tricks for the crew's enjoyment. In this early scene, the Americans and the "others" are segregated in a number of ways. First of all, each group occupies a different space, a space that is presented as "culturally natural." The crew settles down on deck chairs with cocktails in hand to enjoy the performance of the natives, who move so "naturally" in their "natural" playground. This segregation of space is maintained throughout the film: the yacht functions as the site of American (male) civilization and of safety, whereas the island is the site of a primitive paradise, in which gods are female, the local religion is barbarous, and polymorphous perverse sexuality takes the place of Christian sex managed within the confines of monogamous marriage (there are no nuclear families in *Bird of Paradise,* and the only suggestion of marriage is the politically expedient arranged marriage between Luana and the neighboring prince).

When the sharks attack (the first hint that paradise is not all that it is made out to be), Luana, brandishing a knife between her teeth but wearing little else, saves Johnny's life in a daring underwater rescue. Later that night, she sneaks back to the boat to entice Johnny out for an evening swim that turns into a music-and-dance narrative interlude (choreographed by Busby Berkeley) and serves as an erotic mating ritual. This interlude takes place in a kind of "no-mans's land": the ocean functions as unclaimed territory that exists outside of the borders of Luana's or Johnny's societies, which both specify explicit social spaces for romance, sex, and marriage.

A few nights later, Johnny and his friends are invited to attend a celebration on the island. The natives again perform for the crew, this time in a ritualistic dance that turns into mass sexual foreplay. Throughout the performance, the camera divides its time between the gaze of the white men and the bodies of the brown-skinned natives as, one by one, each native man grabs a girl and runs off into the trees. Finally, the only person left dancing is Luana. When she falls to the ground in front of Johnny, he picks her up and proceeds to follow the other men but is immediately obstructed by the local shaman. The yacht's captain, who understands the indigenous language perfectly, tells Johnny that Luana is the chief's daughter and it is "taboo" for any man outside of the tribe to touch her. At the same time *Bird of Paradise* acknowledges the enigmatic desires that cross racial and national boundaries, it immediately sets up miscegenation as a universal prohibition, forbidden by even the most primitive societies.[41]

The initial encounter between the two lovers, initiated by Luana, must be understood within the context of changing gender relations in the United States in the 1930s. New conceptions of marriage among middle-class Americans were confirmed by rising divorce rates, the secularization of the family, and what Dumenil defines as the "emergence of the affectionate family."[42] Along with these familial changes, more women were moving into the workplace. In 1930, 25.3 percent of women over age sixteen worked, up from 20.6 percent in 1900, and 29 percent of married women found jobs outside the home.[43]

However, the move from the domestic economic sphere to the public economic sphere "did not necessarily mean that women enjoyed enhanced equality or liberation" or that this shift was welcomed.[44] Rhona J. Berenstein analyzes the widespread critique of the "new woman," who demanded not only economic and social equality, but access to education and an end to marriage. Berenstein writes that "new women were described in a range of popular discourses as vixens intent on overturning social mores." In order to prevent the disintegration of the American way of life, women "were urged to return to the safety of marriage and maternity."[45]

If at first Luana appears to epitomize a foreign version of this aggressive new woman, she is swiftly recast as the quintessential image of the Western feminine ideal. As an example of what Gina Marchetti characterizes as a "genuine, exotic femininity," uncorrupted by emerging American feminist preoccupations with emancipation, Luana becomes a role model for America's misguided new woman.[46] She is a kind of reconfigured and reformed Eve who, after her initial contentiousness, wants nothing more than to be Johnny's wife and woman, to make a home for him, and to wait patiently for him as he climbs trees and roams the jungle hunting for food, returning each day with the bacon (coconuts in this case). In this role she serves as a warning to women at home: if they don't change their ways, American men will be tempted to turn to "other" woman for satisfaction, threatening the sanctity of Christian marriage as well as the purity of the white American race.

After a brief respite of idyllic domesticity on a paradisiacal island with Johnny, Luana is stolen back by her father to be married off to a neighboring prince. Johnny is captured by Luana's people as he tries to prevent the forced marriage, and the two lovers are condemned to die. Johnny's white male companions must rescue him, for the United States and for the white race, from the savage practices of the brown-skinned natives who are just about to sacrifice the couple to appease Pele, the goddess of volcanoes, who prohibits coupling between races.

Following in the footsteps of Robert J. Flaherty's *Moana* (1926), W. S. Van Dyke's *White Shadows in the South Seas* (1928), and F. W. Murnau's *Tabu: A Story of the South Seas* (1931), the narrative of *Bird of Paradise* labors to transform our original fascination with the island paradise into a perception of it as a menacing space that imperils civilization, capitalism, and the American family. This narrative strategy can be tied directly to a crisis in the United States's perception of itself as a nation bound together by race and history during a time of economic and social instability. This strategy traces its genesis to colonialism, which relied on the notion of racial hierarchy to validate itself. Specifically, through the discourse of racialized sexuality, colonial nations defined their moral as well as their geographic borders.[47]

The South Seas paradise initially offers up for an American audience a temporary escape from the horrors of the Depression. During an era of excessively high unemployment rates and economic hardship, Vidor's film provides visions of a life of ease and plenitude. Although the island natives may lack the material benefits of Western civilization, no one seems to work very hard, there is an abundance of food, and sex is free and plentiful. The space of the island is initially pictured as a beautiful paradise, complete with palm trees, flying fish, gentle waters, and almost-naked, peaceful natives. In a letter to the editor of *Photoplay,* one spectator wrote that *Bird of Paradise,* "with its beautiful scenery of Hawaii, portraying real natives and their customs, left us feeling refreshed and that after all this is a lovely world."[48]

Although the film, like many films of the thirties, makes no direct reference to the stock market crash of 1929, bread lines, unemployment, or homelessness, it spoke to an audience in the throes of economic and social crisis. Through its final depiction of the essentially barbarous nature of "primitive" cultures—natives hungry for redemptive blood, a fiery volcano that physically threatens human life—the film reminded audiences hungry for an escape from the failure of capitalism of the ultimate superiority of Western civilization.

It remains for the narrative to resolve the problem of interracial marriage, which is still a possibility for Johnny and Luana. Aboard the yacht, Luana tends to Johnny, who hovers between life and death, as the crew debates the wisdom of bringing the princess back to San Francisco. The captain reproaches his friends, reminding them that their country is a free one: "Come on, this is 1932. She's a swell girl."

Unfortunately, however, she's not white. Another man warns the captain that he is mistaken. "The boy's whole life is wrapped up in his family. If he brings a native girl home, it will break his mother's heart." The captain concedes, summing up the dilemma with a moral cliché that seemed to serve Hollywood as much as it served the United States in the 1930s: "East is East, and West is West. And never the twain shall meet." East and

West are not merely geographic spaces in *Bird of Paradise*; they also function as signifiers of racial difference and of the inconceivability of race mixing.

Luckily, Luana's father arrives to reclaim his daughter and the crew doesn't have to make the final decision. The captain translates the king's speech for the other crew members: "The volcano curse has been put on Johnny. Unless Luana returns, Johnny will die." Believing that Pele is killing Johnny in order to seek revenge, Luana decides she must sacrifice herself to save his life. She chooses to return to the island with her people. The film's final sequence shows Luana in her royal robe and feathers climbing up toward the volcano's peak, flames superimposed over her. It is clear that she will burn in hell for her sins.

However, Johnny, the white male hero, is acquitted. His male sexual potency is ultimately preserved for his family, his future progeny, the white race, and America. Conversely, del Río's "exotic" sexuality is expendable, not merely because she is a woman, but because she is "not-white." Her racially coded gender serves no productive or procreative purpose. Metaphorically, *Bird of Paradise* reconfigures the Christian parable of origination: the story of Adam and Eve and their expulsion from Eden. In the biblical version, Adam is evicted from paradise for succumbing to the sexual seductions of Woman. In this film, Johnny/Adam must leave the false paradise and return to the "real" Eden, the United States, while Luana/Eve is punished for the sin of seduction.

In most Hollywood melodramas of the 1930s, illicit sexual relationships were often recuperated into the space of familial domesticity. Relations that involved interracial romance had to be managed somewhat differently, however, than liaisons between characters of the same racial designation. Sex was one thing, but the preservation of the Anglo-Saxon American family (both the nuclear family and the national family) was another. The narrative of *Bird of Paradise* makes it clear that although interracial romance might be a fact of life, interracial breeding is definitely not. Despite her love for Johnny, even Luana believes this, proclaiming, "Pele is mad. I have sinned. I taboo for white man." As the *Motion Picture Herald* put it, *Bird of Paradise* is a "daring and exotic romance" in which are depicted "the South Sea's weird savage superstitions and a story of a love that two races tabu *[sic]*."[49] The film's foregrounding of the aberrant nature of miscegenation ultimately forbids sexual relations between Johnny and Luana on the basis of "universal," and therefore "natural," taboos.

I have argued that a cultural ambivalence about race and race mixing in the United States in the 1930s allowed Hollywood to position racially coded stars like del Río as sexual objects within the narrative framework of interracial romance. At the same time, racist ideology precluded films like *Bird of Paradise* from using the conventional resolutions afforded other Hollywood narratives. Films like *Bird of Paradise* and foreign stars like Dolores del Río invoked America's unconscious desire for the other while at the same time reproducing and reconfirming social injunctions against such "perverse" desires and reaffirming American identity as "white."

Despite its depiction of interracial romance, *Bird of Paradise* ultimately prohibits breeding between Johnny and Luana on the basis of cultural taboos grounded in socioeconomic imperatives. The native law reproduces the dominant American prohibition against race mixing and naturalizes it by suggesting that such prohibitions are endemic to even the most "primitive" cultures and the most "heathen" gods. According to this film, Johnny and Luana's desire for each other may be "natural," but the taboo against interbreeding is universal. Although the narrative allows for the possibility that two people from different races may desire each other, the aberrant nature of miscegenation emerges in *Bird of Paradise* as the preeminent, if ambiguous, moral of the film.

For Hollywood, the question of illicit love was a selling point, a promotional strategy that exploited the Westerner's desire for exoticism. In a sense, the film's premise that it is "perfectly natural" for men and women of different cultures and races to desire each other subverts the social interdiction against racial mixing. The production of desire in *Bird of Paradise* thus substantiate's Foucault's claim that sexual normality and perversity are culturally and historically specific.[50]

In films like *Bird of Paradise*, racialized sexuality is deployed in order to naturalize and reinforce other sexual ideologies as legitimate. Depictions of interracial romance are produced in order that they can be set apart, defined as perverse, regulated, and thus controlled. According to Foucault, the purpose of such an "implantation of perversions" is to "ensure population, to reproduce labor capacity, to perpetuate the form of social relations: in short, to constitute a sexuality that is economically useful and politically conservative."[51] For the United States in the 1930s, miscegenation threatened this mandate. In *Bird of Paradise*, Johnny's useful sexuality has to be preserved from the threat of the racial other to ensure the stability of the American "national" family and the preservation of male superiority.[52]

Lea Jacobs argues that the Hollywood industry's self-regulation and self-censorship around issues of sexual representation during this decade constituted a "constructive force, in the sense that it helped to shape film form and narrative" about controversial moral and social issues. Jacobs's contention is that through self-regulation, Hollywood sought to explicate "strategic" responses to social pressures while maintaining its own economic viability.[53] Producers would not willingly jeopardize their economic interests by incurring the enmity of the middle-class, Anglo-Saxon state censorship boards.[54] At the same time, it was apparent that ethnic stars like del Río and interracial romances like *Bird of Paradise* sold at the box office. If Hollywood could, on the surface, market racial otherness as beautiful and erotic, this other kind of eroticism had to be buried beneath the label of a forbidden sexuality.

# 3

## Uncomfortably Real

In the 1930s, del Río starred in a number of films that fell into the category of the "Latin American musical." As Ruth Vasey has suggested, after the introduction of sound, "'foreignness' became less clearly associated with particular ethnic and national groups and became abstracted into an amorphous category of the alien. . . . Even geography became less distinct."[1] The Latin American musicals clearly situated their narratives south of the border. At the same time, the films blurred national and cultural distinctions among various Latin American nations, so that Brazilians wore Mexican sombreros and spoke with Cuban accents while Mexicans danced Brazilian sambas and rumbas and spoke with Castilian accents. In addition, Mexicans portrayed Brazilians and Cubans, and Brazilians were cast as "Latin Americans."

The Latin American musical found success both abroad and at home by exploiting locations that Hollywood considered exotic—Mexico, Brazil, Cuba, and Argentina—as well as "exotic" stars such as del Río, Lupe Vélez, and Carmen Miranda. These films adapted the strategies of anthropological narratives and popular journals like *National Geographic* in order to provide U.S. and European audiences with "pictures" of Latin America. These pictures relied on the appeal of spectacle in the form of exotic costumes and settings as well as ethnic and racial performers who were employed to authenticate Hollywood's vision of exoticism.

Although these musicals were addressed primarily to a North American audience's desire for pure entertainment and exotic spectacle, they were also distributed to one of Hollywood's most lucrative markets in the 1930s and early 1940s: Latin America. Hollywood thus had to take into account the cultural values and desires of its foreign audiences as well as the political and social ideologies of its domestic audience.[2] In trying to do both, the narratives of these films had to maneuver through the land mines of U.S. racist attitudes and practices, land mines that were very often invisible to Hollywood filmmakers.

In this chapter I look at three Latin American musicals starring del Río: *Girl of the Rio* (1932, Herbert Brenon), *Flying Down to Rio* (1933, Thornton Freeland), and *In Caliente* (1935, Lloyd Bacon). I will examine the promotion and reception of these films and del Río's star text in regard to U.S. and Hollywood political and economic relations with Latin American governments and commercial interests. Specifically, I will ask how cinematic representations of racialized sexuality were negotiated in response to Hollywood's dependence on its foreign markets.[3]

Although self-imposed censorship in the form of the MPPDA's Production Code limited filmic representations of sex, crime, and violence, other political and economic pressures also influenced what audiences at home and around the world could view at their neighborhood movie theaters. I argue that representations of race and gender in Hollywood cinema need to be examined not only within the context of political and public discourse but also in relation to pressures of the market during particular historic moments. During the 1930s, the United States faced increasing diplomatic pressure from European, Asian, and Latin American governments to monitor the content of Hollywood films for representations that these governments deemed offensive to their nations and peoples. Given the importance of foreign markets to Hollywood's profit margin, producers could not afford to ignore this pressure.[4]

This argument brings to light some problems with existing studies of the evolution of stereotypes that are concerned primarily with the relation between ideology and representation. The case of del Río evidences the way in which economic and political concerns often compete with ideological ones. The casting of del Río in starring roles in Latin American musicals also illustrates how Hollywood tried to resolve these tensions: the Mexican-born star appealed to Latin American audiences, while her light skin, European features, upper-class role, and star text that recognized her as beautiful by U.S. standards appeased the American public.

## Hollywood in the Depression

When Franklin D. Roosevelt assumed the presidency in March 1933, many U.S. citizens feared the "impending collapse of the American economic and political system."[5] At the time of the crash, the large, vertically integrated motion picture studios, funded primarily by money from Wall Street, were in strong shape. Jack Alicoate, editor of the *Film Daily Yearbook,* noted in his introduction to the 1930 edition that "the motion picture industry enters 1930 in the most prosperous condition in its comparatively short but eventful history."[6] A year later, gross receipts began to fall, but it was not until 1933 that the industry felt the full effects of the crash. Alicoate's introduction to the 1933 yearbook warned that "unless the general economic situation takes a decided change for the better, the industry can hope for little in the way of progress and genuine prosperity."[7] In March 1933, box-office receipts "were 40 percent of what they had been in January of 1931."[8] Hollywood had to respond to and contest both the economic indicators and the public's mood to reclaim audiences and recover from the disastrous effects of the Depression. The primary tools it had at its disposal were its films, its stars, and its cultural links with the U.S. public.[9]

The studios seem to have understood the pulse of their exhibitors and their audiences, who demanded from Hollywood during this critical period, above all else, entertainment. Judging from box-office records during the Depression, the public wanted to be released from, rather than reminded of, the social and economic realities of everyday life, and film producers and directors were more than willing to produce, package, and sell their particular brand of utopian liberation.

Aside from adverse economic conditions, in 1931 Hollywood confronted another constraint in the form of the self-imposed code of "Don'ts and Be Carefuls" discussed in chapter 2. The Depression brought additional moral pressures to bear on Hollywood as religious and other conservative groups lobbied local and national leaders to implement more restrictive measures. In response, the Motion Picture Production Code, a set of moral "standards" written by Martin I. Quigley, the Catholic publisher of the preeminent trade magazine, the *Motion Picture Herald,* and Daniel A. Lord, a Jesuit priest, was established in 1930 and revised in 1934. The Code did not proscribe sex and crime in the movies—as Robert Sklar points out, that would have been the death of the motion picture industry.[10] Instead, it set the conditions, the moral standards, according to which sex and crime could be represented. Hollywood succeeded in meeting these conditions and, in the process, realized an economic victory that would pull the industry out of the Depression.

One of the genres that seemed to satisfy both the public's desire for entertainment and the restrictions imposed by the Production Code was the musical, which "came of age" in the 1930s. According to Thomas Schatz, in response to the overwhelming success of MGM's Academy Award-winning *Broadway Melody* of 1929, "hundreds" of musicals were produced in the 1930s.[11] On the surface, the musical was the most logical means of exploiting cinema's newest technology, sound. However, the genre consists of more than movies with lots of music: musicals are narratives into which music and show business and the notion of groups of Americans working together are fully inscribed. This ideology fit with the philosophy of the political and social goals of the Roosevelt administration, which was charged with "fostering a spirit of patriotism, unity and commitment to national values."[12] According to Giuliana Muscio, during the Depression the dynamism of Hollywood musicals "acted as an antidote. . . . They mobilized a physical response to the social paralysis, valorizing the chorus—'the people' and productive organization."[13]

Hollywood marketed the musical and the public understood the genre as "pure entertainment."[14] In popular discourse, entertainment was seen as a means of "escape" from the conflicts of everyday life and "wish fulfillment" through entertainment's visions of utopia. Richard Dyer defines cinema's utopian sensibility as the "capacity of entertainment to present either complex or unpleasant feelings . . . in a way that makes them seem uncomplicated." For Dyer, musicals offer the following "utopian solutions": abundance, energy, intensity, transparency, and community.[15]

More significantly, as Ella Shohat and Robert Stam have argued, through its staging of a utopian "evocation of social harmony," Hollywood's musical genre, in general, "has articulated ethnic heterogeneity . . . through music and dance."[16] Although nonwhite racial and ethnic groups rarely figured as major players in the narratives of the musical, foreigners and racial others provided background "color" and spice in the musical numbers that structured these films. This "background" material, however, proved problematic for one of Hollywood's most important audiences: Latin America.

In the 1930s, Latin America was Hollywood's third most important film market after its home audience and Europe.[17] Of all films exhibited throughout Latin America, 90 percent were produced in the United States.[18] The effect of the Depression on foreign economies precipitated a drop in theater attendance in Latin America as well as the closing of many theaters. This loss of box-office revenues south of the border was worrisome for American producers and distributors. To make matters worse, Hollywood had to contend with the growth of film industries in a number of Latin American countries, primarily Mexico and Argentina. In 1930, the introduction of sound technology advanced these national industries and threatened Hollywood's dominance.

One of Hollywood's responses was to produce more than one hundred films in Spanish. For the most part, these "Hispanic" films were Spanish-language remakes of English-language films. Despite Hollywood's best attempts, Latin American audiences rejected the Hispanic films. They wanted to hear their own Spanish accents, not those of Spain or Los Angeles, and they resented the stereotypical and false cultural representations Hollywood offered up in these films.

Foreign markets had always been important, not only for the revenues they generated for the film industry, but for the ways in which Hollywood films enlarged the markets for other mass-produced goods.[19] U.S. film companies did not operate in isolation from other economic and political institutions. The industry, represented by its trade association, the MPPDA, enjoyed tacit cooperation, as well as oversight, from the federal government early on. The establishment of the Motion Picture Section in the Bureau of Foreign and Domestic Commerce in 1925-26 secured support for Hollywood's expansion into international markets. Then, in 1933, newly elected President Franklin D. Roosevelt announced his intention to broaden the bureau's scope south of the border.

Studio distributors stationed in Latin America advised their companies that they could do "a tremendous business if we could get them to insert some Spanish dialogue in their pictures."[20] Hollywood developed a number of film projects that employed Latin American themes, places, and stars. Given the importance of the Latin American region to U.S. political goals, studios were constrained by the Department of Commerce to make their stories about and representations of Latin American nations and people "acceptable." And, as noted above, Hollywood did not want to jeopardize foreign box-office profits by antagonizing those audiences.

Despite these restraints, exotic stereotypes "continued to prove irresistibly attractive to producers."[21] Shohat and Stam define exotic stereotypes as "tropes of empire" and remark on how they tend to focus on stars' bodies, most often the bodies of women. Latin American women were associated "with verbal epithets evoking tropical heat, violence, passion, and spices. Thus Lupe Velez becomes 'the Mexican Spitfire,' Acquanetta the

'Venezuelan volcano,' Olga San Juan the 'Puerto Rican pepperpot,' Marie-Antoinette Pons the 'Cuban hurricane.'"[22]

One only has to look at publicity materials from del Río's musicals to see how studios relied on these "tropes of empire" to market their Latin American stars and films. For example, a headline in a 1934 issue of *Photoplay* tells us, "Dolores Extols Passive Love." The article goes on, "Her golden skin, smooth as mellowed ivory and her dark, flashing eyes bespoke the lure of those maidenly 'senoritas' who peep at life from behind cloistered shutters. . . . When the young man comes to call on a senorita in Mexico . . . he brings his guitar."[23]

A promotion still from *Wonder Bar* (1934, Lloyd Bacon), in which del Río plays an undifferentiated Gypsy-like Latina dancer, features del Río in an embrace with costar Ricardo Cortez (an Austrian Jew born Jacob Krantz who changed his name to take advantage of the public's fascination with "Latin lovers").[24] Describing the embrace, the photo's caption reads: "The passive manner—Dolores is touched by the Latin technique Ricardo Cortez uses in this amorous scene." Another promotion for the same film declares that "old Mexico, with its star-strewn skies and brooding mountains, its age-touched haciendas and orchid-grown jungles, is a perfect setting for such a languorous romance."[25]

A *Photoplay* story features a picture of del Río wearing a low-cut dress and lots of eye makeup: "Meet the Duchess, otherwise the exotic Dolores Del Rio. . . . Contrast her dark loveliness to the blond Jean Harlow across the page and you'll know why Hollywood wins the world's beauty sweepstakes without any trouble."[26] Although, as noted above, the "lightness" of del Río's skin color was emphasized in articles about her beauty, at the same time much of Hollywood's promotional material in the 1930s focused on her "dark loveliness," *darkness* being a synonym for other women who were set in opposition to American blonds like Harlow.[27] It was her films, however, that most forcefully presented the young star to audiences at home and abroad as "other."

## Girl of the Rio

Del Río's first Latin American musical, RKO's *Girl of the Rio*, was a talkie version of the play and silent film *The Dove*, discussed in chapter 1. In a rare role as a Mexican woman, del Río plays Dolores Romero, "the Dove," a singer at the Purple Pigeon, a questionable nightclub in a fictitious town on the Mexico-Texas border called Mexicana. Norman Foster stars as Johnny, who works across the street in a small gambling house, the Club International, and is in love with the Dove. Leo Carrillo is Don Jose Maria

*A representation of "Latin" lovers: del Río and Ricardo Cortez in* Wonder Bar. *Photograph courtesy of the Museum of Modern Art, New York.*

Lopez y Tostado, who is constantly informing everyone that he is "the bes' damn caballero in all Mexico."

The original silent version of *The Dove* was one of a number of films banned in Mexico in the 1920s. The Mexican consul general, G. S. Seguin, accused Hollywood of "using grossly exaggerated and very negative Mexican characterizations."[28] The Mexican government instituted an embargo against Famous Players and Metro in response to films like *The Dove*. However, that embargo proved difficult to enforce and relatively ineffective.[29] Mexican exhibitors rallied against the quarantine, arguing that it hurt their business, which, at the time, was dependent on the screening of Hollywood films. During the 1920s, according to U.S. Department of Commerce Reports, "Hollywood films provided between 75 to 85% of Latin American total Motion picture consumption."[30]

Hollywood did not invent stereotypical images of Mexicans. They appeared in early American travel literature and nineteenth-century western dime novels. These characteristics, readily understood by the mass audiences of early cinema, were adapted to portray cinematic Mexicans. The political and ideological effects of the Spanish-American War of 1898 also affected the earliest U.S. cinematic representations of Mexico and Mexicans, intensifying existing negative perceptions.

An Edison Kenetoscope travelogue titled *Pedro Esquirel and Dionecio Gonzales: Mexican Duel* was one of the first films that imaged the Mexican stereotype. Mexican stereotypes proliferated in films such as *The Greaser's Gauntlet* (1908, D. W. Griffith), *The Mexican's Jealousy* (1910), *On the Border* (1913), *Bronco Billy and the Greaser* (1914), *The Greaser* (1915), and *Scarlet Days* (1919, D. W. Griffith).[31]

World War I, the decline of European markets, and expansion of Latin American markets resulted in the discontinuation of the use of the word *greaser*, at least in film titles.[32] However, the end of the war and the reemergence of vital European markets also saw the return of negative stereotypes of Mexicans and other Latin Americans.

Margarita de Orellana argues that Hollywood was not "trying to suggest that all Mexicans were like those represented on the Screen. Their object rather was to present the Mexican as a representative foreigner, to give the 'other' a shape and form."[33] The "shape and form" of this other, however, was predicated on dominant ideologies of the racial "difference" and perceived racial characteristics of "the Mexican." In Hollywood films, this difference was imagined as racialized sexuality: Mexican male characters in the silent Hollywood cinema were dark-skinned, swarthy mestizo (mixed-blood) "greasers," whereas Mexican women were generally docile, sensual, and light-skinned, with Spanish (European) rather than Indian or mestizo features. De Orellana remarks that although this other woman may "belong to a higher social class [than the men], she remains culturally and racially inferior to the North American."[34] These stereotypes persevered in early sound films such as *Girl of the Rio*.

In this film, the nation of Mexico is depicted as a barely civilized frontier that exists just over the U.S. border. It is a landscape of small, poor towns filled with nightclubs that function as thinly disguised brothels, disreputable gambling establishments, and haciendas occupying vast expanses of land owned by ignorant, wealthy Mexicans who speak with fake greaser accents and are interested only in women, alcohol, and money. Mexico responded as vehemently to this second version of *The Dove* as it had to the first. Officials considered *Girl of the Rio* to be "offensive" and permitted it to be "exhibited only in a censored version."[35] Mexican officials ultimately prohibited the distribution of the film in Mexico on the basis of the negative portrayal of Leo Carrillo's Don Jose. Del Río apologized to her country for her role in the film. Apparently, she had insisted that the action take place somewhere in the Mediterranean, but was overruled by RKO.

While *Girl of the Rio* goes out of its way to paint del Río's character as feminine and virtuous, it also plays into the conventional stereotypes about Mexican women. Although she was in her thirties by the time the film was made, del Río's Dove comes across as a sweet and naive young girl who speaks broken English with a "cute" foreign accent that immediately

*Hollywood's version of Mexican masculinity and femininity in* Girl of the Rio. *Photograph courtesy of the Museum of Modern Art, New York.*

connects her racially with the greaser caballero Don Jose, who speaks with the same funny accent. (Interestingly, a Chinese gambler who frequents the Club International speaks with the same accent.)

Simultaneously, the narrative positions del Río as attractive to and available for the white male hero. The cultural borders that separate race seem to play out in the same way as the permeable geographic border of the dusty street that separates the United States from Mexico: as a clear-cut line that is nonetheless easily traversed if necessary.

Race, on the surface, is textually repressed through the representation of romantic relations between Johnny and Dolores and through Don Jose's affiliation with the "bad" white men who want to use the girl as a trading commodity. However, like all repressions, race haunts the text in innumerable ways. Thus, although the Dove is a "good" and "acceptable" Mexican, as evidenced by the way in which she is marked with "positive" stereotypical traits (virtue, goodness, the desire to sacrifice herself for the white man), all the other Mexicans are identified by "negative" stereotypical attributes (swarthiness, dishonesty, and violence), attributes that are accentuated to a parodic level in the character of Don Jose, who is overweight, dark-skinned, and sports a long moustache and big sombrero.

Although the film was not a box-office success, RKO did not blame it on del Río and immediately cast her in *Bird of Paradise*. Vidor's big-budget film made a lot of money for RKO and restored del Río's star status. She was given a leading role in another RKO film, *Flying Down to Rio*, opposite Gene Raymond. This film marked the debut of Fred Astaire and Ginger Rogers and was the first in a series of RKO musicals that featured the dancing duo.[36]

Del Río stars in the role of Belinha, a Brazilian heiress who meets and falls in love with a wealthy U.S. band leader, playboy, and amateur stunt pilot named Roger (Gene Raymond) at a nightclub in Miami. By sheer coincidence, Roger's band is invited down to Rio de Janeiro to inaugurate the opening of a new hotel owned by Belinha's wealthy father, Señor de Rezende. When the hotel's grand opening (and its future) is threatened by greedy capitalists from an unnamed European nation, the band operates as the cultural arm of the U.S. government. Under Roger's direction, the Americans save Señor de Rezende from certain ruin by staging a spectacular performance in the air with Ginger and a chorus of showgirls mounted on the wings of stunt planes. While dealing in international intrigue, Roger wins the hand of Belinha, who had been engaged to one of his best friends, Julio, a wealthy Brazilian.

*Flying Down to Rio* is typical of the Hollywood backstage musical,

*Rich Brazilian woman falls for poor American man in the utopian resolution of* Flying Down to Rio. *Photograph courtesy of the Museum of Modern Art, New York.*

which interweaves a romantic plot with the trials and tribulations involved in the mounting of a theatrical musical. According to Schatz, the musical genre's "gradual narrative progression toward a successful show and the principal performers' embrace, project a utopian resolution" of the conflict between "object and illusion, between social reality and utopia." Specifically, Schatz proposes that these films offer their audiences "utopian visions of a potentially well-ordered community."[37]

The well-ordered community of *Flying Down to Rio* happens to be an "imagined community" of nations committed to transnational capitalism, engendered through a history of economic and cultural imperialism. Despite the fact that by the 1930s Brazil's population was primarily Afro-Brazilian and poor, this film presents the Brazilian community as white and wealthy. Dark-skinned Brazilian characters function in the same position as dark-skinned Americans do: as "colorful" and secondary background material rather than as fully formed characters whose roles are central to the film's narrative. For example, in a musical scene that features the popular carioca, Brazilian dancers are segregated into a group of white couples who perform a Westernized dance routine and a group of black couples who perform a "native" dance. The "native" dance is immediately colonized by Astaire and Rogers, who are intent on proving that they can do the carioca better than any Brazilian. A critic for *Variety* suggested that the choreographer (Dave Gould) "probably could have had a lot of fun if they'd let him cut loose with the colored folks."[38]

At the conclusion of *Flying Down to Rio,* Belinha rejects Julio for the blond, white hero. Like a number of films of that period, this film advertises interracial romance. However, unlike those other films, it also seems to condone miscegenation in the face of U.S. racist attitudes—Belinha and Roger intend to be married and, given the function of marriage in the 1930s, most probably to propagate. *Flying Down to Rio* thus allowed the romance to come to the conventional Hollywood narrative closure, whereas films like *Bird of Paradise* killed the nonwhite love interest. The difference in the narrative resolution of these two films may be attributed to the fact that in *Bird of Paradise* del Río plays a dark-skinned "savage princess" from a non-Christian South Seas tribe, whereas in *Flying Down to Rio* her character is a light-skinned, upper-class woman, the daughter of a wealthy, Europeanized Brazilian capitalist.

The discrepancy in the films' endings could also, however, be ascribed to the importance of the Brazilian market to RKO's distribution networks and the relative unimportance of the Pacific markets in the 1930s. Consider that the narrative of the film tells the story of a North American cultural envoy (the band) coming down to save a failing Brazilian commercial enterprise from shadowy fascist figures. The film thus unabashedly promotes Roosevelt's policy of Pan-Americanism and free trade. In choosing her American boyfriend over her Brazilian fiancé, del Río's character reinforces this narrative and political project. According to Brian Henderson, Belinha functions as "sometimes a displacement of the [colonial] desire for Brazil, sometimes its embodiment."[39] Although Henderson is speaking of Belinha as an erotic "(imperialist) object of desire," as a metaphor of Brazil, she is also an object of political and economic desire.

Sérgio Augusto points to a number of elements related to both the production and the content of *Flying Down to Rio* that evidence the political and economic parameters of film production and promotion. First of all, the project was initially proposed by Lou Brock to the head of RKO, Merian C. Cooper (director of *King Kong*). Cooper was also on the board of directors of Pan Am Airlines, which was expanding its routes in South America.[40] In one scene, Belinha and Roger send wires to Rio de Janeiro via RCA Communications, a business partner of RKO.[41] Second, the film's release coincided with Franklin D. Roosevelt's introduction of his Good Neighbor Policy in 1933.

The Good Neighbor Policy embraced economic, political, and cultural strategies in an effort to assuage anti-U.S. sentiments that had been in place in Latin America since the Spanish-American War. It was also intended to temper growing isolationist sentiments in the United States that were threatening business interests in Latin America. FDR was motivated by pressures to expand U.S. markets in Latin America during the Depression and was convinced by businessmen that Hollywood films sold U.S. products. Finally, the Good Neighbor Policy aimed to sell "Americanism" in order to counter the growing Axis commercial and ideological influence in the Latin American region as World War II geared up in Europe.

Producers therefore had to be careful about how their films represented Latin Americans. A letter from Dr. James Wingate of the MPPDA to the producer of *Flying Down to Rio,* Merian C. Cooper, evidences this concern. Wingate notes that "we also feel that the dialogue on page 30 by Belinha, 'That's how nice girls are brought up in my country. Complete supervision from . . . how do you say it? . . . infancy to adultery,' will be resented by the South American people."[42] The Production Code Administration (PCA) approved the film on July 21, 1935, only after RKO complied with a request to "tone down" the carioca dance "and to remove the offensive sex suggestiveness."[43]

At the same time, the dominant discourse around questions of race also influenced the PCA's concern with the film. In a letter to Sidney Kramer of the RKO Distributing Corporation, the PCA suggests that "the entire colored troop, with the exception of the finale, might well be dispensed with."[44] Although the Brazilian population might be predominantly mixed-race, apparently "coloreds" were superficial to official U.S. conceptions of community.

Despite the success of *Flying Down to Rio,* RKO did not renew del Río's contract. However, Warner Bros. signed her up immediately for a starring role in another Berkeley musical, *Wonder Bar.* Warner Bros. hoped "she would bloom into another Garbo," the Swedish star who was under contract to Metro-Goldwyn-Mayer.[45] *Wonder Bar,* with Al Jolson, Dick Powell, Ricardo Cortez, and Kay Francis, is a kind of musical murder mystery imbued with racial subtexts. Del Río plays Gypsy dancer Ynez, who works with her partner Harry (Cortez) in Jolson's club, the Wonder Bar. Ynez is in love with Harry, but he is a small-time gigolo involved in an affair with a rich man's wife, played by Kay Francis.

This film offers up numerous examples of what Michael Rogin calls cinematic "racial cross-dressing." According to Rogin, the practice of "racial cross-dressing" was an "Americanizing" exercise that facilitated the assimilation process for "white" immigrant filmmakers and spectators. It transformed "ethnic identity into an American national identity," disassociating those who were "100% American" from those who were not.[46] At the same time, the masquerading of ethnic identity "deliberately mobilized identity exchange—between colored and white, man and woman, ethnic and American." For Rogin, racial masquerade in the cinema was a productive cultural practice that created certain visible relations of power based on racial identification.[47]

Jolson's performance in *The Jazz Singer* (1927) is probably the most famous instance of racial cross-dressing. In *Wonder Bar,* he reprises his Jew-in-blackface role in a Busby Berkeley number for his wealthy white audience. This performance begins with him singing to a child who is also in blackface, "Ever since I was a little pickaninny" and ends with "I'll be glad to see Abe Lincoln like he used to be. The man who set us free." When Jolson knocks at heaven's pearly gates, he's greeted by a black St. Peter, a black Gabriel, and a band of black angels. Ole Black Joe plays on his banjo as the angels show him around heaven's hot spots, including "Pork Chop Orchard" and "Possum Pie Grove," where Uncle Tom eats fried chicken. This scene is performed entirely by whites in blackface for an audience of wealthy white patrons.

Although Jolson's masquerade may have been "self-assertive, ethnic self-mockery," this role was generally not available to most racial and ethnic stars.[48] In the same film, del Río also performs a cross-dressing masquerade as a Mexican in the role of a Spanish Gypsy. In one scene, she dances against a backdrop of a chorus of blond women made up in matching black gowns and blond wigs. They are joined onstage by a dance troupe of blond women and dark-haired men. Del Río's "dark" Ynez complicates this black-and-white motif: she is neither a blond woman nor a dark-haired man. In *Wonder Bar,* and in each of her other Hollywood films, del Río's role-playing is doubly conflicted. She is a racial and national other masquerading as a racial and national other. Unlike the racial identities of Al Jolson in *The Jazz Singer,* Judy Garland in *Babes on Broadway* (1941), and Jennifer Jones in *Duel in the Sun* (1946), del Río's racial identity will not wash off.

Neither *Wonder Bar* nor del Río's next picture, *Madame DuBarry,* did as well as the RKO films.[49] Warner Bros. returned her to the Latin American musical genre as a dancer named Rita Gomez (alias "La Españita") in *In Caliente,* a musical set in Caliente, Mexico, starring Pat O'Brien, Edward

*Racial cross-dressing: Al Jolson in* Wonder Bar. *Photograph courtesy of the Museum of Modern Art, New York.*

Everett Horton, Glenda Farrell, and Leo Carrillo. The film was part of a series produced by the studio with the choreographer Busby Berkeley that included *42nd Street, Gold Diggers of 1933,* and *Footlight Parade. In Caliente* did reasonably well at the box office but did nothing to further del Río's career despite aggressive publicity on the part of Warner Bros.

The studio relied on stereotypes about Mexico and Mexicans to promote the film. Confusing Mexico with Spain, promotional material advertised the dancing in *In Caliente* as "a new spanish custom . . . its torrid! Its Tropical! . . . Seething with senoritas" (actually blonds in black wigs). "Warner Bros.' Flaming Filming of Mexico's Million Dollar Paradise of Girls, Song and Laughter."[50]

The *Motion Picture Herald* reported that a number of theaters sponsored a "'Caliente Night' Ball or Party, Lets Debs Go Hotcha for Charity. . . .

In Caliente *"seethes with señoritas." Del Río as "La Españita." Photograph courtesy of the Museum of Modern Art, New York.*

Notables go in Mex costumes." The writer suggests "tieups with Mex, Styles, Foods. . . . Restaurants might advertise mex dishes, like Chili Con Carne and the like." Warner Bros. offered three "life-sized, hand colored figures" for lobby displays and a new service, "Rent-a-Costume. . . . The woman's costume consists of a laced mantilla and beautiful gown. Men receive a sombrero, trousers, bolero jacket and shirt."[51]

A script for a radio spot was published that has del Río and Pat O'Brien driving down to Mexico:

> O'BRIEN: Look, what is that down there blocking the road?
> DEL RIO: It is a cart, such as our peons use.

O'Brien yells at the owner of the cart, Pedro Gillermo Teresa San Isidoro y Pinares del Monte, to move his cart while del Río suggests, "Perhaps he do not understand English." Pedro, who happens to be armed like all Hollywood Mexicans, replies: "I unnerstan the Eenglish. Steeck 'em up! Queeck."[52]

*Photoplay* included *In Caliente* among the "Best Pictures of the Month," along with *Public Hero No. 1* and Shirley Temple's *Our Little Girl.* *Variety* noted that "for the Latin territory, Miss Del Río alone insures it a strong box office draft."[53] In addition to the film's promotion, five feature articles on del Río in *Photoplay* coincided with the opening of *In Caliente,* all of them focusing on her "dark beauty": "Pick makeup 'to fit' face, is Del Rio Tip"; "'Naturalness is the keynote of modern mode in makeup,' explains Dolores del Rio"; "Means that every woman should select very carefully the shades best suited to her inherent type of beauty." "'Cleanse Face Nightly' says Miss Del Rio. 'In my own case, as you can see, my skin is dark and dry.'" "Dark, dry skin care explained by del Rio." "The dark, dry skin needs a cream foundation." Another *Photoplay* article foregrounds del Río's upper-class foreignness: "Luncheon at Dolores Del Rio's . . . Flower Bowl—hand made antique Mexican. Service Plates and Bread and Butter Plates—Sterling hand-made by Sojihe in Mexico with crystal from Bullocks and China from England."[54]

Unable to come to a contractual agreement with Warner Bros., del Río made one film for Columbia Pictures, *Devil's Playground* (1937), playing a Mexican dancer, the "catty" Carmen, who weds one man and seduces his best friend. The role of the femme fatale realigned her with the negative stereotypes of Mexican women. A reviewer for the *Hollywood Reporter* described del Río's Carmen as a "Mexican minx . . . the "predatory Mexican." According to the reviewer, del Río "has a part that exactly fits her talents and her looks. She is uncomfortably real."[55] The reviewer's comment reveals an unconscious fear submerged below the American audience's fascination with this Mexican star. While for almost twenty years Hollywood had worked to promote del Río as an "acceptable" other, the visible presence of an undeniably foreign body constantly reminded the public and the industry that the "problem" of race could not categorically be effaced.

When *Devil's Playground* flopped, del Río broke her contract with Columbia and moved back to 20th Century Fox, where she starred in three films: *Ali Baba Goes to Town* (1937, David Butler), *Lancer Spy* (1937, Gregory Ratoff), and *International Settlement* (1938, Eugene Forde), in which she plays a French singer in a film about the bombing and military devastation of Shanghai during the Sino-Japanese war. She returned to Warner Bros. for *I Live for Love* (1935), another Berkeley musical, in the role of a temperamental South American stage star. According to the *Hollywood Reporter,* the film was "put together for the display of Dolores del Rio's exotic charms and the pleasing baritone of Everett Marshall."[56]

In 1940, del Río had a small, supporting role in the Metro-Goldwyn-Mayer Civil War western *The Man from Dakota.* That same year, she divorced her second husband, Cedric Gibbons, and began an affair with the young director Orson Welles while he was in the midst of producing *Citizen Kane* (1941). Welles gave her a leading role in *Journey into Fear* (1942), an espionage film he wrote and codirected, which was reedited by RKO and released to disparaging reviews. Soon after, Welles abandoned del Río for another "Latin" beauty, Rita Hayworth (née Rita Cansino), whom he wed in 1943. Devastated, and with her star status in decline, thirty-eight-year-old del Río returned to Mexico with her mother to become one of the foremost Mexican stars of the Golden Age of Mexican cinema.

The Latin American market continued to be crucial to Hollywood's profit margin. By 1938, Hollywood's European audience was in sharp decline in response to the Spanish Civil War, Hitler's rise to power, stricter censorship regulations in Europe, and higher import tariffs. Nathan Golden, director of the U.S. Commerce Department's Film Division, advised the industry to continue to pursue the Latin American market, which still accounted for 10.6 percent of Hollywood's foreign revenue.[57] Hollywood relied, in part, on the Latin American musical well into the 1940s, with films like *Down Argentine Way* (1940), with Betty Grable, Don Ameche, and the Brazilian star Carmen Miranda; *Weekend in Havana* (1941), starring Alice Faye and Carmen Miranda; and *Road to Rio* (1947), starring Bing Crosby, Bob Hope, and Dorothy Lamour.

In these and other films, the industry continued to reproduce cinematic stereotypes of Latin American nations and subjects. Ultimately, behind the facade of Berkeleyesque musical numbers and international romance lay a complex discourse about U.S. national identity, an identity that was partially predicated on notions of racialized sexuality. But, as I have argued, using the case of del Río as example, in representing this discourse, Hollywood studios had to walk a fine line between concern for profits in foreign markets and the goodwill of audiences at home.

# 4

# "Nuestra Dolores"

While her Hollywood career flourished in the 1920s and 1930s, del Río refused requests to perform in Mexican films.[1] Her reluctance can be ascribed to multiple factors: her success in Hollywood, the instability of the Mexican film industry, the relatively low salaries stars in Mexico commanded, and her concern about her reputation in Mexico.

Mexicans who emigrated to the United States were often denounced in Mexico. The derogatory label *pocho* branded those who were perceived to have abandoned their Mexican heritage and assimilated themselves into U.S. culture.[2] Del Río was not unaware of the strained relations between Mexicans and Mexican Americans. In chapter 3, I discussed the hostility she faced in Mexico in response to her role in *Girl of the Rio* in 1932. Mexican audiences and the Mexican government condemned that film for its insulting portrayal of Mexicans and castigated del Río for taking part in the offense. That experience influenced her later professional decisions. In 1934 she refused an offer to star in MGM's *Viva Villa!*, another Hollywood version of the Mexican Revolution. When the film was finally released (with Fay Wray in the role of Villa's lover), it was boycotted by Mexican filmmakers and intellectuals for its spurious portrayals of Pancho Villa and the Revolution.[3]

In 1934, the weekly *Todo* (similar in style and content to *Life* magazine) ran an interview of del Río by Gabriel Navarro (who also wrote for the U.S. Spanish-language paper *La Opinión*). When Navarro asked her to explain her unwillingness to take part in *Viva Villa!*, she responded, "Por razones de mexicanismo [For Mexican reasons]." According to Navarro, she turned down the role of Villa's love interest because she did not want to appear "unpatriotic" or "anti-Mexican."[4] That same year, during a visit to Mexico after a nine-year absence, she assured her compatriots, "I return as Mexican as when I left Mexico."[5]

In 1942, when del Río set up residence with her mother in Coyacán, a fashionable suburb of Mexico City, Mexico was experiencing the beginnings of its "economic miracle" and Mexican cinema was enjoying its "Golden Age."[6] Due to state support, film was the third-largest industry in the nation, and domestic film production grew from six films in 1932 to fifty-seven films by 1938.[7] In 1943, the year that del Río appeared in a Mexican film for the first time, seventy films were released. By the early 1940s, the Mexican film industry boasted a solid financial and industrial base; seasoned producers, directors, and film technicians; and a star system that attracted a domestic audience.

Although much of the industry's growth was due to state economic policies and to Latin America's continued demand for Mexico's Spanish-language films, some of the industry's success must be attributed to the recognition by Mexican producers and directors that their prosperity depended on a loyal national public. This public was, first and foremost, interested in being entertained by genres, stories, and stars they recognized as "Mexican." However, the cinema of Mexico served a larger purpose than simple entertainment during its Golden Age. As Carlos Monsiváis puts it, the public looked to cinema to "explain how to survive in a bewildering age of modernization . . . to find and experience entertainment, family unity, honour, 'permissible' sexuality . . . and to understand how they belonged to the nation."[8] And it was the movie star who embodied for the spectator the visual link to the cinematic nation that was portrayed on neighborhood screens.

The star system in Mexican cinema had been slow to develop. The nonfiction genre dominated Mexican cinema during the first two decades of the century. These early films celebrated the nation by documenting its landscapes, its indigenous cultures, and the political pomp and circumstance of the nation's capital. Although a few fiction films were produced, using actors from Mexican theatrical traditions, dramatic filmmaking came to a virtual standstill during the Mexican Revolution (1911–17). By

1910, the majority of films screened in Mexico were imported, primarily from France.

The end of the fighting and the growth of economic and social stability reopened a space for the launching of a Mexican studio system and Mexican feature-film production. However, by the 1920s, Hollywood dominated Mexico's motion picture screens and Mexican production remained at very low levels throughout the 1920s and early 1930s. The limited frame of Mexican silent cinema did not permit the development of sustainable acting careers or the emergence of a star system.

The introduction of sound technology allowed Mexico to develop a cinema that appealed to its audiences at home and in other Spanish-speaking Latin American countries. At the same time, the development of well-equipped film production studios in the 1930s (bankrolled by private investment, government loans, and U.S. money) fostered the expansion of production.[9] The increase in the number of films provided opportunities for a number of actors to become celebrities. By the early 1940s, Mexican producers realized that Mexican movie stars were profitable commodities that could be used to market their films.[10] Sara García, Jorge Negrete, Pedro Infante, and the comedian Cantínflas, had emerged as the most popular, visible (and highest-paid) stars.

In 1943, the year del Río appeared in *Flor silvestre,* an article that highlighted "the most featured Mexican female stars in the last ten years" named Andrea Palma, Consuelo Frank, Esther Fernández, Margarita Mora, Lupe Vélez, Isabella Corona, Marina Tamayo, Mapy Cortés, and Susan Guízar as the "most popular and prestigious stars in Mexican films."[11] Just two years later, another survey found that two women who were not on the above list now ranked as the nation's favorite female stars. These two women were María Félix and Dolores del Río.

Félix appeared in her first two films in 1942 *El peñón de las ánimas* (Miguel Zacarías), opposite Jorge Negrete, and *María Eugenia* (Felipe Gregorio Castillo), but her star status was not affirmed until *Doña Bárbara* (1943, Fernando de Fuentes). Whereas Félix's star text was initially formed within the economics and aesthetics of the Mexican film industry, del Río's had to be remanufactured. Despite her nationality, del Río was a Hollywood movie star. Monsiváis suggests that "if in Hollywood she was asked to be *deeply spontaneous* (that is, 'primitive') . . . in Mexico, this 'exotic flower' will be allowed no such spontaneity": she was required to perform with deliberation the role of a moral Mexican woman.[12]

Both *Flor silvestre* and *María Candelaria* allowed her to discharge this role, reinvented her as a "Mexican" movie star, and made her a favored celebrity in the eyes of her Mexican audiences.[13] In *Flor silvestre*, Fernández's allegorical melodrama of the Mexican Revolution, del Río stars as Esperanza, a young peasant girl. The narrative encapsulates the national mythology of the Revolution within the tragic love story of two people from different social classes whose doomed love gives birth to a new Mexico and the new Mexican in the form of their son.[14]

In flashback, Esperanza recounts this story for her son, now a young military cadet. The story begins when Esperanza falls in love with José Luis Castro (Pedro Armendáriz), the son of wealthy *hacendados* (landowners). Despite his high-class status, José Luis is an idealistic supporter of the Revolution's objective of bringing political, economic, and social justice to the underclasses. His parents reject Esperanza because she is from the peasant class, and the Revolution because it threatens the foundation on which their wealth and status rest. However, the couple secretly marries and their child is born at the outbreak of armed conflict. When José Luis runs off to join the Revolutionary forces, a pair of bandit brothers, posing as Revolutionary soldiers, murder his father and take Esperanza and her son hostage. José Luis returns to rescue them but is killed in front of his wife and son.

*Flor silvestre* is part of a national transformation of Mexican Revolutionary rhetoric, a transformation that continues today. The end of Cárdenas's presidency in 1940 and the shift to a more conservative administration marked the political conclusion to the Mexican Revolution. Although the Revolution's mythologies "continued to lend legitimacy to Mexican governments in the second half of the twentieth century," successive administrations used those mythologies to justify their increasingly conservative policies.[15] Manuel Avila Camacho (1940–46) linked his programs of increased modernization and industrialization to the legacy of the Revolution with the following explanation: "Each new era demands a renovation of ideals. The clamor of the Republic demands now the material and spiritual consolidation of our social achievements, by means of a powerful and prosperous economy."[16]

If the political and economic priorities of Mexico were changing, its ideological grounding in the "Revolutionary family" persisted.[17] Indeed, the discourse of the national family remained one of the enduring ideologies of post-Revolution administrations, both liberal and conservative. The ideal of a nation bound together by a shared history is still the primary "foundational fiction" of the modern Mexican nation.

In actuality, the Revolution and the ensuing process of urbanization and industrialization affected Mexican families in profound ways. The

*The construction of post-Revolutionary Mexican femininity: del Río in* Flor silvestre.
*Photograph courtesy of Cineteca Nacional, Mexico City.*

traditional extended family structures of rural peasants and Indians were
torn apart as family members moved to the cities in search of work.
Changing gender roles inspired by political and economic transformations
challenged conventional patriarchal structures of family life as women
entered different sectors of the labor force and the Catholic Church lost its
firm hold on family and national life.

Numerous films throughout the 1940s pictured this changing family in various generic disguises.[18] In family melodramas such as *Cuando los hijos se van* (When the children leave; 1941, Juan Bustillo Oro) and *Una familia de tantas* (A family among many; 1948, Alejandro Galindo), the drama of an evolving nationalism is played out in stories of urban, middle-class Mexican families undergoing personal crises.[19] The *comedia ranchera* romanticized the pre-Revolution family of the feudalistic hacienda, a family composed of white *hacendados,* mestizo lieutenants, and Indian serfs.

*Flor silvestre* challenged the reactionary tendencies of both the family melodrama and the *comedia ranchera.* Fernández's film is fully committed to a Revolutionary ideology that seeks to create a new Mexican family that will incorporate previously disenfranchised groups: the lower classes, Indians, and women. *Flor silvestre*'s mythic family is, in essence, what Jean Franco describes as "the holy family of the post-Revolutionary state."[20] In the film, the old aristocratic family is destroyed as another, temporary family rises up from its ashes. *Flor silvestre* acknowledges that this new structure is transient: it functions long enough to produce an heir and is then destroyed to make a space for the emergence of the modern, post-Revolutionary Mexican family.

*Flor silvestre* established del Río and Armendáriz as the "first couple of the Mexican cinema," and, by extension, the representation of the first couple of the new Mexican family.[21] Del Río successfully discharged the role of the national feminine archetype, and Armendáriz personified the paternal nation as the quintessential male Revolutionary hero figure who sacrifices his life for his family and his country.

*Flor silvestre*'s Mexican premiere was devastating for del Río. Outside of her friends and numerous journalists, very few people attended the film's opening in the Palacio Chino. The reviewer for *Hoy* suggested that the film was just another story about a love affair between a wealthy *hacendado* and a simple peasant girl and that the public would not find it at all a novelty.[22] Distraught, del Río attributed the rejection to the public's memory of her participation in *Girl of the Rio* ten years earlier.[23]

However, thanks to an aggressive publicity campaign that promoted the film's and the star's excellence, del Río's reputation was redeemed. By the following week, critics were calling the film "masterly" and "the best film made in Mexico in recent years." The painter Diego Rivera, a close friend of the actress, agreed and declared that this was the Mexican film that he had been waiting for.[24]

Del Río received an Ariel (Mexico's equivalent to the Oscar) for best female actress and the Mexican audience embraced her as their own star.[25]

*The "first couple of Mexican cinema": Dolores del Río and Pedro Armendáriz in* Bugambilia. *Photograph courtesy of Cineteca Nacional, Mexico City.*

Most significantly, her performance was heralded as the "incarnation of the female Mexican peasant," a role she would recapitulate in her next film, *María Candelaria*. Ironically, as with many of her earlier Hollywood roles and her Hollywood star text, this peasant analogy contrasted sharply with her public persona as it was promoted in the Mexican media. During her Hollywood career in the 1920s and 1930s, the Mexican press and popular weekly journals such as *Todo* and *Hoy* featured articles on del Río. She was pictured as an excessively modern woman, appearing in the social pages or in regular cinema columns wearing the latest Paris and New York fashions and entertaining artists, politicians, and movie stars from both sides of the border in her Los Angeles home.[26]

Throughout the 1940s and 1950s, the media continued to emphasize her wealth, her "modernness" and cosmopolitan taste, her fashionable lifestyle, and her prominent circle of friends and lovers. Despite her appearance in films as a peasant, an Indian, and a prostitute, del Río remained the epitome of the modern bourgeois woman for her Mexican public. This woman strengthened Mexico's conception of itself as a modern nation.

The imaging of the modern Mexican woman in fashion magazines and newspapers announces that she did share some qualities with her European and North American counterparts. This resemblance can be connected to the transnational distribution of the ideologies and commodities of style and fashion, disbursed through popular culture and Hollywood films, which still dominated Mexican screens.[27] It can also be related to Mexico's perception of the United States as the industrial model of modernity.

However, there were other images that cannot be so easily linked to Euro-American ideas of the "modern woman" but were specifically aimed at distinguishing the new *Mexican* woman, a woman with whom Mexican citizens could identify. This modern Mexican woman was a subject of considerable discussion in newspapers and other periodicals as well as in film. Journalists and public figures debated daily the shifting terrain of gender roles and relations. As with other conversations about the "modern woman" around the world, the categories that were under discussion were those that identified her visually—by her looks, her fashion, her hair—as well as those that defined her social self: in Mexico these were, most significantly, her sexual morals, her place in the home and in public, and her gendered national identity. I want to emphasize that this modern Mexican woman was both mythical and real. Her mythology was tied to historical and legendary constructions of woman and to specific social and political projects of post-Revolution Mexico.

The modernist project of Mexico was grounded in a twenty-year concerted effort toward profound political, economic, and social progress. Over this period, and through successive presidential administrations, an agriculturally dependent, rural-based population with linguistic, class-based, racial, and historical divisions and only indeterminately bound together by politics and the recent history of the Mexican Revolution was made into a new nation. This nation was forged through revolutionary violence and committed to the hegemonic construction of a modern, multiethnic, multicultural nation and national citizen. This new social order required new subjects and new social relations, new kinds of men and women, and new models of gendered relations.

Real women from various social strata were being moved and moving themselves into this modernity. But as a product of cultural and ideological imaging, the modern woman was also a fabrication of individual and social imagination and desire. What did this modern woman look like? She often resembled her U.S. and European contemporaries, favoring slinky black evening dresses, New York and Paris fashions that barely covered her knees, and French berets that snugly fit her short new bob. This woman was middle-class, slender, athletic, light-skinned, and European looking. She was the personification of "feminine elegance" and Parisian "chic," the image that del Río performed in her public life.

However, the majority of Mexican women did not fit the above description of the modern woman. In 1940, only 15.5 percent of the population were middle- or upper-class; 84.5 percent occupied the lower socioeconomic strata. By 1950 those figures had shifted to 27 percent and 73 percent, respectively.[28] This other modern Mexican woman lived in the sprawling suburbs of Mexico City after having recently migrated there from rural areas and small towns. She often worked outside the home but did not yet have the right to vote in national elections (that came in 1953).[29]

Additionally, the majority of these "other" women did not resemble the white, aristocratic "lady" personified by del Río in the society pages; many of them were but a generation removed from the "peasant" girl del Río represented in *Flor silvestre* or the Indian maiden in *María Candelaria*. It was this gap between the "real," historical woman and the image of the "modern" woman that fed the public's fantasy of stars like del Río.

Like Hollywood, Mexican cinema took part in the circulation of contemporary discourses about racial and national identity. Race was a central, though implicit, component of Mexico's post-Revolution search for a common national identity.[30] Mexico's population had been racially mixed since the Spanish Conquest of the sixteenth century.[31] Race as a signifier of breeding or blood was subsequently used to differentiate among criollos ("white" Mexicans who claimed European ancestry), Indians, and mestizos (Mexicans of "mixed" blood). Post-Revolution politicians and intellectuals aspired to forge an identity that superseded any apparent racial, ethnic, or historical differences. Their purpose was to construct an "authentic" Mexican culture by either incorporating or erasing diversity.

One of the most far-reaching philosophies promoted during this era was *indigenismo*, a network of intellectual and political ideas that called for a unified national identity under the banner of a common Indian heritage. Proponents of *indigenismo* argued that the roots of modern Mexican identity—*lo mexicano*—lay in the cultural legacy of the pre-Columbian Indian cultures whose populations were devastated during the prolonged Spanish Conquest. Although *indigenismo* purported to recognize the fundamental contribution of Indians to Mexican culture, its champions often failed to acknowledge linguistic, historical, and cultural differences, and even variations in racial stock among the diverse groups that made up Mexico's indigenous populations.[32]

*María Candelaria,* del Río's second film with Fernández (who was of Indian ancestry himself), belongs to the Mexican genre of "Indianist" films that promoted *indigenismo* by elevating the Indian to mythic status. In 1935, two government-sponsored films—*Redes* (Nets), codirected by Fred Zinnemann, Paul Strand, Augustin Velázsquez Chávez, and Emilio Gómez Muriel; and *Janitzio* (starring a young actor named Emilio Fernández), directed by Carlos Navarro—inaugurated the genre.[33] A decade after the release of *Redes* and *Janitzio,* Fernández revived the indigenist genre with films like *María Candelaria, La Perla* (1945), *Enamorada* (1946), *Maclovia* (1948), and *Río Escondido* (1948).

In *María Candelaria* (essentially a remake of *Janitzio*), del Río plays a young Indian woman rejected by the people in her village, who believe she violated their sexual mores by posing nude for a painter. She represents the archetypal and mythohistorical virgin/whore polarity of Mexican femininity: the Virgin of Guadalupe, Mexico's patron saint, who stands in for the ambiguous figure of the maternal virgin, and La Malinche, an Indian woman sold to the Spanish by her own people who eventually became Hernán Cortés's mistress and his interpreter and who was denounced as a traitor to her country by subsequent generations.[34]

*María Candelaria* has been denounced by various Mexican critics for raising Indians to mythic stature, romanticizing their poverty-stricken lives and, following the model of the earlier films, linking the idea of a pure Mexican national identity visually and narratively to Mexico's indigenous roots. The painter in the film (standing in for Fernández, who perceived his role as that of the creator of Mexican national cinema) declares that his mission is to "paint Mexico." In the body of María Candelaria he has found what he calls "an Indian of the pure Mexican race. . . . It was as if an old princess had come to judge the conquistadors." In *María Candelaria,* the themes of history, nation, and woman are tied together by Fernández's lyrical style and the film's mythical references to pre-Columbian Mexico. Through the cinematographic modeling of Figueroa, del Río's face takes on the lines and planes of the museum sculptures of Mexico's pre-Columbian races.[35]

In the opening sequence of the film, a series of shots links statues of Mexico's pre-Columbian Indian to the living face of a contemporary Indian. This sequence is often compared to the images in Sergei Eisenstein's unfinished film, *¡Que viva Mexico!* It is common knowledge that one of the major influences on the aesthetic development of Mexican cinema was the Soviet director.[36] In 1932, funded by the American writer Upton Sinclair, Eisenstein traveled to Mexico to make a film about Mexican history.[37] The photographic images of Mexico that Eisenstein and his cameraman, Edward Tisse, constructed reemerge in *Redes,* in *Janitzio,* and in the films of Fernández and Figueroa in the form of Indian faces, expansive cloud-filled skies, and impoverished landscapes.[38]

Numerous scholars and reviewers have criticized the casting of an "international" star like del Río in the role of an Indian who is supposed to represent "the pure Mexican race." Mexican film historian Aurelio de los Reyes writes that, like its "Indianist" predecessors, *María Candelaria* "attempts to reevaluate the beauty of the Indians, but such intention is contradicted by the presence of professional actors in the central role; the authentic Indians . . . were reduced to the role of extras." He brands del Río a "sacred monster of Hollywood" who returns to Mexico only to revitalize her flagging career and argues that the "glamorization" of the Indian, through the casting of del Río, only works to preclude authenticity.[39]

However, it is a mistake to assume that audiences in Mexico confused the mythology of films like *Flor silvestre* and *María Candelaria* with history, or that they failed to understand that del Río was only impersonating an Indian. First of all, the "history" that these films present falls under the rubric of what Marcia Landy terms "common sense history," which is a history that "reflects and refracts images from the past and the present."[40] It is a history that is fashioned daily by those who must make sense of what the past means for *their* social, cultural, and political present.

Although an "official" past may be articulated by those in power for institutional, ideological, commercial, or policy-making objectives, other pasts are formulated by individuals and social groups out of the material offered to them through national myths and legends, through educational pedagogy, and through popular culture. As Landy puts it, although historical films are "open to the criticism of at least simplifying and even of falsifying history . . . the language of these films feeds on the multivalent nature of everyday life and touches on prevailing conceptions of nation, gender, sexuality, and ethnicity."[41]

Second, the idea that *hacendados* could fall in love with poor peasant girls might have been utopian, but it did explicate a powerful belief that perhaps class barriers could be effaced. Such convictions were grounded in everyday lives imbued with hope and "everyday strategies of survival."[42] Rather than read del Río's aristocratic star text as conflicting with the official "primitive" nature of the Indian, audience members in Mexican movie theaters could experience in del Ríos's performances the nobility of María Candelaria's Indianness or the transgressive strategy of conquering class barriers in *Flor silvestre.*

Like film audiences everywhere, Mexicans understood the allegorical nature of the cinema and indulged in the pleasures and fantasies that films provided. In her study of female spectatorship, Jackie Stacey explores this particular practice of cinemagoing. She found that women viewers recognize both the "similarities and differences" between themselves and the glamorous, mythical characters they saw on the screen. Stacey quotes viewers who say, for example, "I don't think I consciously thought of myself looking like any particular star . . . it was more the semi-magical transformation of screen identification."[43] In the case of the elegant del Río, Mexican women realized that they could never "be" del Río, but they enjoyed the fantasy of the temporary identification that her screen presence afforded them.

*María Candelaria* received national and international recognition and put Mexican cinema on the international map. It was the first Mexican film to be recognized at Cannes in 1946 and garnered critical acclaim for its director, its cinematographer, and its stars. Del Río and Armendáriz were crowned the preeminent cinematic couple, and they reappeared together in a number of films under the direction of Fernández. *María Candelaria* confirmed del Río's position as one of the two "leading ladies" of the Mexican cinema. For the next decade, she and María Félix played significant roles in interpreting the agenda of feminine beauty and culture in Mexico.

## The Other Modern Woman

As suggested in the above discussion of *Flor silvestre* and *María Candelaria,* Mexican cinema of the 1940s responded to changes in women's social and economic roles. Numerous films that focused on female protagonists evidenced the difficulty of incorporating these material changes into popular discourse. The *cabaretera,* or "dance hall," films of the 1940s, for example, narrated stories about women supporting their families in one of the few lucrative positions available to Mexican women. Called *las ficheras,* many of these women, who were in fact prostitutes, were depicted as self-sufficient characters who often managed to rise above their fate. *Fate* is the operant term here, because these women were, for the most part, depicted as sympathetic characters, good women forced into a bad life due to circumstances beyond their control.[44]

Del Río's next film, *Las abandonadas* (Abandoned women; 1944), recounts the story of one of these women and provided a different vision of femininity for her audience, one that offered up other possibilities of identification. Another collaboration among del Río, Fernández, and Figueroa, and also starring Armendáriz, *Las abandonadas* is a descendant of one of the first successful Mexican sound films, *Santa* (Saint; 1931, Antonio Moreno). *Santa* was based on a novel by Federico Gamboa and starred Lupita Tovar in the role of a young country girl who is seduced and abandoned by a handsome soldier. Forced to seek refuge in one of the many brothels in Mexico City, Santa becomes a much-sought-after prostitute. In a few short years, however, she dies from the effects of poverty, alcoholism, and disease. According to Monsiváis, the character of Santa "explained, justified, and anticipated . . . and essentialized the destiny of women in Mexican melodrama." This woman would embody the qualities of silent suffering, sacrifice, passivity, and self-denial that Santa incarnated. For Monsiváis, this "monstrous" woman was definitively personified by Dolores del Río in many of her Mexican films.[45]

As Margarita, del Río assumes the role that Lupita Tovar gave birth to in *Santa*. As a poor but honest young girl, a pregnant Margarita is abandoned by her lover. She eventually marries a wealthy general but is forced to become a prostitute when he dies. Her redemption comes in the form of maternal sacrifice.

Del Río, who had just turned forty, successfully managed the responsibility of portraying a young girl, a middle-aged prostitute, and an elderly woman and received another Ariel for her accomplishment. In contrast to her previous two roles as an Indian woman and a peasant woman, in *Las abandonadas* del Río enacts yet another type of Mexican woman. Margarita is a kind of "Stella Dallas," a woman who transforms herself numerous times throughout her life in order to survive and raise her young son to be a successful lawyer. These transformations span the first forty years of the twentieth century, tracking for the film's audience Mexico's shift from the Porfirian dictatorship, through the years of the Revolution and post-Revolution nation building, and into the presidency of Avila Camacho. Thus, although it is not one of Fernández's explicitly "Mexicanist" films, *Las abandonadas* does exemplify the director's troubled vision of the Mexican Revolution and its legacy.

One of the legacies of the Revolution was the reformation of Mexico from a rural, agriculturally based country into one defined by an unprecedented degree of industrialization. Industrialization was accompanied by profound reorganization of social structures and relations. Among other changes, Mexican women faced significant alterations in many facets of their lives. At the same time, other discourses demanded that they preserve traditional values of femininity, which included submissiveness and chastity. As Margarita, del Río embodied post-Revolutionary national and gendered transformations in the role of a national (female) citizen who sacrifices herself for the welfare of the new Mexican nation, represented in the figure of her son.

Despite the film's moral ending, *Las abandonadas* was censured for its "sexual explicitness," and authorities initially refused to allow it to be

*Maternal sacrifice: as a seduced and abandoned woman, del Río relinquishes her life for her son in* Las abandonadas. *Photograph courtesy of Cineteca Nacional, Mexico City.*

exhibited unless certain suggestive scenes were cut. When it was finally shown, it was very successful at the box office and well received by both critics and audiences.

While waiting for the authorities to release *Las abandonadas,* del Río made one more film with Armendáriz, Figueroa, and Fernández, an expensive costume melodrama, *Bugambilia.* After this fourth film with Fernández, she went to work for another director, Fernando de Fuentes, in *La selva de fuego* (Jungle of fire; 1945), a disturbing exploration of sexual repression. Del Río plays Estrella, a beautiful adventurer who appears unexpectedly at a gum tree plantation in the Yucatan jungle and is confronted with a group of men who have not seen a woman in more than six months.[46]

In 1946, del Río worked with yet another director, Roberto Gavaldón, in a film written by the respected Mexican writer José Revueltas. In *La otra,* del Río plays a dual role of twin sisters, María and Magdalena (a very thinly disguised reference to the biblical Mary and Magdalene, the virgin and the whore).[47] María is a jealous manicurist who kills her sister, who has married a wealthy man, and assumes her place.

For the next few years, del Río enjoyed the prestige of being one of the most successful film stars in Latin America. In 1948 she starred in an Argentinean film, *Historia de una mala mujer* (Luis Saslavsky), based on Oscar Wilde's play *Lady Windermere's Fan.* In 1949 she turned forty-five and, although she was still beautiful, could no longer play youthful roles. Her subsequent films featured her as an "older" woman, still beautiful but no longer able to compete with younger women. In *La malquerida* (1949, Fernández), for example, del Río stars as Señora Raimunda, the owner of a large hacienda, whose second marriage to a younger man (played by Armendáriz) is resented by her daughter, Acacia.

In 1950, del Río received an Ariel for best actress for her role as another older woman in *Doña Perfecta* (1950, Alejandro Galindo). Based on a novel by the Spanish writer Benito Pérez Galdós, the film is set in nineteenth-century Spain. Del Río plays Doña Perfecta, an exceedingly religious woman who watches over the morals of the town of Santa Fe. Her nephew (Carlos Navarro), an atheist and champion of Darwin's theory of evolution, falls in love with Doña Perfecta's daughter, Rosario (Esther Fernández).

Monsiváis maintains that "from *Doña Perfecta* on, she only plays Dolores del Río, the filmic and social institution."[48] She had no choice. A new breed of modern women dominated the Mexican cinema and offered up new definitions of Mexican femininity that del Río could not fulfill. Del Río was limited to certain roles because of her age and because of the institutionalization of her star text as a woman who was traditional and timeless, common and aristocratic, beautiful and passive. The new female Mexican star occupied a modern site. She personified the young, middle-class urban woman who could be sensual and seductive.

More significantly, the new Mexican star assumed an alternative purpose that was less ideological and more functional. According to Gustavo García, female stars exhibited a sensuality that was more "grounded" in the reality of the urban middle class, "less elaborated and artificial." The new paradigm of female beauty—broad hips, ample breasts, pronounced waist, wide shoulders, frank smile, large eyes, full cheeks—was exemplified by young stars such as Joan Page, Mary Esquivel, and Elvira Quintana.[49]

The transformation of Ninón Sevilla from *Aventura en Río* (1951) to *Maratón de baile* (1957) "marked the gradual but unrestrained separation between the already-tested potential of the stars and the new conditions of functionality that was at the service of a financially depressed cinema."[50] During the 1940s, the Mexican government had supported the film industry. Miguel Alemán's administration (1946–52) established a new bank, the Crédito Cinematográfica Mexicano (CCM), to help finance the nation's largest film producers. The CCM quickly moved into production and distribution, buying up studios and movie theaters. The government also instituted a number of protectionist measures that supported the establishment of state distribution with the institutionalization of Películas Nacionales, S.A., in 1947.

These actions were not enough, however, to prevent the subsequent decline of Mexican cinema in the early 1950s, in terms of both quality and quantity. After the war, the United States withdrew its support for the Mexican film industry, which had an immediate effect on Mexican cinema. Production output dropped from 72 films in 1946 to 57 in 1947.[51] Eduardo de la Vega Alfaro suggests that in response to this decrease, Mexican film-makers "discovered a formula for survival and consolidation: the production of low-budget films based on urban-suburban themes."[52] These films, and the new actors and actresses who inhabited them, became extremely popular with the new urban lower-class audience. An average of 102 films were produced per year between 1948 and 1952 and kept the industry afloat during a time of increasing crisis.[53]

In 1952, President Adolfo Ruíz Cortínes's administration centralized film production, distribution, and exhibition and instituted additional measures to reduce the number of foreign films allowed into Mexico to 150 per year. As a result, film production levels remained consistent—83 films in 1953, 118 in 1954, and 136 in 1958.[54] However, Mexican critics agree that this came at a price—that of quality, as producers turned to tried-and-true formula pictures to draw audiences and ensure profits.

Throughout the 1950s and 1960s, del Río starred in a number of lower-budget films, including *Reportaje* (1953, Fernández), *El niño y la niebla* (1953, Galvadón), *Señora Alma* (1954, Bracho), *¿A dónde van nuestros hijos?* (1956, Alazraki), and *La cucaracha* (1958, Rodríguez), with her rival, María Félix. *La cucaracha* was one of a number of films that reenvisaged the Revolution and the Revolutionary heros that sustained Mexico's vision of itself. For Monsiváis, Rodríguez's film was a "historic farce . . . where the armed struggle served only as a pretext for the histrionic duels of the sacred monsters of the Mexican cinema: María Félix and Dolores del Río, Pedro Armendáriz and 'el Indio' Fernández."[55]

The "duel" between Félix and del Río had been institutionalized by the Mexican public in the press. A few years earlier, in 1949, a well-known Mexican journalist asked a number of Mexican writers to rate these two stars on the basis of ten attributes, including elegance, talent, beauty, personality, and box-office appeal. Del Río collected 670 points, whereas Félix, who at thirty-one was ten years younger than del Río, received 580 points.[56]

Onscreen, the duel was played out in the visual, ideological, and narrative structures of *La cucaracha*. Del Río portrays a "decent beauty" opposite Félix's Revolutionary *soldadera* (female soldier). Visually, del Río is passive and submissive. In the role of the devoted wife of reactionary town politico, she leans on the arm of her husband, moving quietly and demurely across the screen or, alternately, throwing herself into the uncontrolled abandon of a hysterical woman.

Félix's role as the *soldadera* transformed by love and sexual passion is a caricature of the *soldadera* in Matilde Landeta's *La Negra Angustias* (1949). Landeta's film, adapted from a novel by Francisco Rojas Gonzales, narrates the story of a young mulatta (María Elena Marquez) who becomes a revolutionary *coronela* of a small Zapatista army.[57] Landeta's *soldadera* is willful and aggressive, and although the majority of cultural representations focus on the *soldadera*'s sexuality and on discourses about femininity, gender equality, and gender roles, *La Negra Angustias* problematizes these questions. Landeta's film exposes the failures of a revolution that promised social and economic equality for all of Mexico's citizens.[58]

*La cucaracha*, on the other hand, mocks the *soldadera*'s version of womanhood while celebrating traditional forms. Félix, the *soldadera*, is loud in voice and appearance, overbearing, and assertive. She wears pants, a hat, guns, and bandoliers and drinks and smokes as much as any man. She swaggers like a macho and sits down decisively in her chair, legs spread in a sexually confident manner. Her sexuality is willful, vital, and demanding. Félix's *la coronela* likes her sex intense and violent.

Del Río's woman, however, is loyal to her husband and to his politics. Her black attire contributes an aura of virginity to her character. Her sexuality is moral and hidden. Monsiváis describes her in this and other films as lacking "will-power."[59] *La coronela* is reduced to femininity through a single sexual encounter with a "real" macho when Emilio Fernández, in the role of Antonio Seta, a Pancho Villa clone, brings her literally to her knees. The incident immediately transforms her into a "female" woman who wears dresses and jewelry and walks hand in hand with her revolutionary lover through a town in the throes of Revolution.

Earlier films about the Mexican Revolution were successful vehicles for the portrayal of an important post-Revolution ideal: the Mexican male hero. The fabrication of a revolutionary machismo had a calculated function. Although this new form of machismo may have shared certain tenets of male superiority with previous forms of patriarchal practices—aggressive sexual and social behaviors and wife beating, for example—what gave it its specific quality was its association with Mexican nationalism and its "officialness, its openly proclaimed status as part of the national identity."[60] The celluloid revolutionary hero was the quintessential macho.

As discussed above, the on screen personas of all of these stars were developed early on in their careers in Mexican cinema. Félix became a top Mexican star with her portrayal of the vengeful Doña Bárbara, who dresses in men's clothing, takes on the aggressive and paternalistic manners reserved for the Mexican male, and rides astride her horse like a man. Following the success of the film, Félix's star text was defined by the beautiful but evil and aggressive female characters she played in films such as *La mujer sin alma* (1943, Fernando de Fuentes), *La devoradora* (1946, de Fuentes), and *La mujer de todos* (1946, Bracho).

Del Río, on the other hand was always the malleable, eternally suffering woman. *María Candelaria, Flor silvestre,* and *Las abandonadas* confirmed that role for her. If Félix fashioned her own star text, according to Monsiváis, del Río was always in the service of the directors she worked with: "Gavaldón will make her the Virgin of Melodrama; Galindo will use her in his unusual anticlerical enterprise, and 'el Indio' Fernández will see in her the undefilable object of his nationalism."[61] Despite the intentions and machinations of her directors, however, for her Mexican public, she was always "Dolores del Río," a symbol of an unattainable vision of Mexican femininity; she was *nuestra Dolores*.

# 5

# Mexico Is a State of Mind

*Suddenly one felt an impatience with all this mummery, all this fake emphasis on what is only a natural function; we die as we evacuate; why wear big hats and tight trousers and have a band play? That, I think, was the day I began to hate the Mexicans.*

Graham Greene, *Another Mexico*, 1939

In 1947, at the age of forty-four, del Río accepted an offer from John Ford to star in *The Fugitive,* a Mexico-U.S. coproduction based on Graham Greene's novel *The Power and the Glory.*[1] The film tells the story of a priest, played by Henry Fonda, who attempts to flee an unnamed Latin American country during a violent confrontation between government forces and the Catholic Church. Del Río's character, a young unwed mother named María Dolores, helps the priest to escape after he baptizes her fatherless child.

Although U.S. film critics panned the film, they applauded del Río's performance, praising her for her "fine-boned face," for being "beautiful and restrained as the barefoot Mary Magdalene who helps [the priest] to escape," and for being "sad, beautiful, but not overly stimulating."[2] In other words, she was acclaimed for satisfying American expectations of Mexican femininity.

*The Fugitive,* and del Río's role in the film, offers an opportunity to think about Hollywood's construction and *use* of Mexico in the 1940s as well as a means to interrogate the function that Mexico served for the U.S. postwar imagination. In the following discussion, I examine *The Fugitive* as a filmic translation of two colonial subjects: Mexico as an imaginary geographic and political space, and del Río as a cinematic figure who embodied, for Ford and for Hollywood, Mexico as a feminized and colonized space. Through complex processes, Mexico, the "source," is displaced onto the body of del Río, the "rendition," through multiple mediating processes, including novelistic and filmic conventions as well as conventions of representing female others.

At the same time, I argue that the postcolonial relation between Hollywood and Mexico was not merely one of domination and subjugation. Mexico was (and had been for a century) an active participant in the U.S. and Hollywood understanding of "otherness." I therefore consider the extent to which Mexico and Mexican cinema contributed to Hollywood's rendering of Mexico into a "recognizable" form.

## Writing Mexico

The English author Graham Greene wrote *The Power and the Glory* after visiting Mexico in 1937 and 1938, basing it on his published travel diary of that experience.[3] The diary, *Another Mexico* (originally title *The Lawless Roads*), is a form of the genre Mary Louise Pratt identifies as "sentimental travel writing."[4] Travel writing promotes a particular kind of translation, one that explicitly places the self in the center of an other's space. Although Pratt situates sentimental travel writing in the context of "late eighteenth-century crises in Euro-imperialism," the mode figures prominently throughout the nineteenth and twentieth centuries and is made visible in ethnographic and fiction films.

Purportedly "about" Mexico in the late 1930s, *Another Mexico* must also be read as an account of Greene's struggles with his own faith and political beliefs and with his feelings about Mexico and Mexicans. Greene's biographers have, in fact, noted that in his work, "the normal distinction between fiction and reality repeatedly broke down."[5] Throughout the diary, Mexico and the Mexican people emerge as a product of a self that "hated" the country. If at first Greene finds the Mexican peasants to be "the population of heaven," and is "ready to think of Mexico in terms of quiet and gentleness and devotion,"[6] he soon "begins to despise these people." Greene writes, "The intense slowness of that monolithic black-clothed old woman with the grey straggly hair—removing a tick. . . . People never seem to help each other in small ways."[7]

According to Greene, *Another Mexico* is about the "religious situation" of a country he hates, a country he finds to be suffused with "disappointment and despair." A fervent Catholic convert and a disillusioned former member of the Communist Party, Greene concludes that all the problems he encountered in Mexico could be attributed to the fact that no Catholic masses had been said in the capital in ten years and to the policies of "the blue-chinned politicians on the balcony, the leaders of the state, with their eyes on the main chance, the pistols on their hips, with no sense of responsibility for anyone at all."[8]

Unlike ethnographies, personal narratives make no pretense to what James Clifford calls "constructed domains of truth, serious fictions."[9] In the travel diary, the self that writes is called upon to give the reader his or her own personal vision, to imbue that vision with emotional and "personal" responses, and to make sense of all experience within a frame of reference known to that self. *The Power and the Glory* is obviously not a fictional account of the diary. Instead, Greene's novel presents the reader with his diary's private "structure of feeling," which is translated into the guise of historical fiction. *The Power and the Glory* became the novelized version of personal experience in which the author/traveler's subjectivity is displaced onto the quasi-fictive persona of a priest.

In the beginning of *Another Mexico*, Greene briefly recounts the true story of a Jesuit priest, Father Miguel Pro, who returned to Mexico in 1926 upon completion of his religious training in a European seminary: "We know how he was dressed when, a year and a half later, he came out into the prison yard to be shot, and he may well have worn the same disguise when he landed." Father Pro was executed during what Greene calls the "fiercest persecution of religion anywhere since the reign of Elizabeth."[10] The persecution to which Greene refers was known as the Cristero Revolt (1928–32), a protracted series of skirmishes between government troops under President Plutarco Elías Calles and an unlikely alliance of landless Catholic peasants and conservative landowners in the northwestern regions of Mexico. Right-wing landowning groups, or *hacendados,* opposed the post-Revolution socialist land reforms instituted by Calles and expanded upon by the next president, Lázaro Cárdenas.

The Catholic Church and its congregation of Catholic peasants rose up alongside the *hacendados* against the state's anticlericism and its socialist programs. The bloody revolt lasted almost four years and resulted in the loss of eighty thousand lives. The peasants were fiercely Catholic, in the traditional sense of the practice, and combined their fervent Catholicism with fervent patriotism, fighting under the red, white, and green flag of independence with "the Virgin of Guadalupe on one side and the eagle devouring the serpent on the other."[11]

Although both the novel and the film take place within the context of a fictionalized account of this political battlefield, their narratives are explicitly about man's troubled relationship with God. For Greene (and subsequently for Ford), the confrontation between the Church and the state became a battleground for a contest for authority over "the spirit of the peasant."[12]

## Picturing Mexico

*The Fugitive* was Ford's first independent film made through his production company, Argosy Pictures, in association with RKO Radio Pictures. He had attempted to produce the picture before World War II but could not secure financing. Even after the war, the picture only got made with the backing of Mexican state and film industry officials. Shot in Mexico at the Churubusco Studios (partly owned by Howard Hughes and RKO), *The Fugitive* was coproduced by Merian C. Cooper (producer of *King Kong* and *Flying Down to Rio*) and del Río's Mexican director, Emilio Fernández. Fernández's longtime cinematographer, Gabriel Figueroa, worked on the picture, as did a number of Mexican-born actors, including Pedro Armendáriz, Leo Carrillo, Miguel Inclán, Rodolfo Acosta, Fortunio Bonanaova, Chrispin Martin, Fernando Fernández, José Torvay, Enriqueta Reza, and Columbia Dominguez.

In *The Fugitive*, the battle for the soul of the Mexican peasant is played out between the fascist state, symbolized by the fanatical police lieutenant (Armendáriz), and the "common man," portrayed by Henry Fonda's doubting priest. This battle was mediated by the Church, embodied in the figure of del Río's María Dolores.

María Dolores is an ambiguous character who projects complex and confused notions of Mexican femininity and of U.S. understandings of Mexican femininity. Her moral traits and her physical appearance are borrowed from Mexican cinema's construction of Mexican woman as outlined in chapter 4. As I have argued, this construction was an amalgam of artistic, ideological, and cinematographic imaginings: Mexican Catholicism's vision of femininity, Diego Rivera's and David Siqueiros's murals of a gendered Mexican post-Revolutionary nationalism, Eisenstein's cinematic ethnography of Mexico, and the gendered nationalistic philosophies of post-Revolution nation builders such as José Vasconcelos, Samuel Ramos, and President Lázaro Cárdenas. This complex figure was then modified according to Ford's own Catholic understandings of female and cinematic purity, and in response to Hollywood's entrenched version of what a Mexican woman looks like and acts like. The production of *The Fugitive* and of del Río's Mexican woman in the film is thus an effect of transnational collaboration.

J. A. Place remarks on the visual style of *The Fugitive*, writing that it is

*Hollywood's construction of Mexican femininity in* The Fugitive. *Photograph courtesy of the Museum of Modern Art, New York.*

"the most expressionistic style [Ford] has ever used . . . the angles, lighting, and composition . . . sometimes look like Eisenstein's most symbolic work."[13] The film's visual resemblance to Eisenstein's work is not, however, coincidental. As I discussed in chapter 4, Ford's coproducer, Fernández, and his cinematographer, Figueroa, were inspired by the Soviet filmmaker's sojourn in Mexico and his posthumous film *Que viva México!* (1932).

Fernández and Figueroa incorporated Eisenstein's visual, editing, and representational strategies in the design and structuring of their films. *The Fugitive,* under the influence of Fernández and Figueroa and their assistants, replicates many of these aesthetic strategies to construct its vision of a historical moment in an "unnamed" Latin American country.[14] Tag Gallagher discusses one of these moments in the film: a shot, reverse shot, sequence of the police lieutenant and his prisoner. Gallagher notes that "the opposing internal angles of frames 1 and 2 interlock with an interesting dynamism."[15] This quality of dynamism is intrinsic to Eisenstein's theories of composition and of montage and to Figueroa's cinematography.

Ford's earlier work was also influenced by Eisenstein's cinema. Gallagher labels Ford a "Hollywood expressionist," placing him alongside "*realist-*

expressionist" directors F. W. Murnau and von Sternberg and in opposition to "*expressionist*-realist" filmmakers Eisenstein, Fritz Lang, and Alfred Hitchcock.[16] Although Gallagher acknowledges that "each director mixes" the two modes of filmmaking, he argues that, in general, the second group "tends to pursue relatively monolithic goals and to aim for sensation rather than for reflection," a quality he assigns to the "*realist*-expressionist" directors.[17]

According to Gallagher, Murnau's *Sunrise* (1927) was the formative influence on the development of Ford's aesthetic style.[18] At the same time, Gallagher argues that Ford's relation with his audience "is due to dialectical tensions at almost every level: between audience and film, between themes, emotions, compositional ideas. Not surprisingly, the 'typical Ford shot' is a geometric depth in which people stare at each other across space."[19] In point of fact, these dialectic and geometric visual and editing practices are central to Eisenstein's films and to his film theory.[20]

An analysis of the cinematic strategies in *The Fugitive* reveals that

*The visual style of Mexican director Emilio Fernández and cinematographer Gabriel Figueroa was influenced by post-Revolutionary Mexican art and by the work of Soviet filmmaker Sergei Eisenstein. Here, Dolores del Río and Pedro Armendáriz in* The Fugitive. *Photograph courtesy of the Museum of Modern Art, New York.*

*Ford's "expressionist" vision is evident in this composition and lighting treatment in*
The Fugitive. *Photograph courtesy of the Museum of Modern Art, New York.*

many of Eisenstein's influences are still at work in Ford's aesthetic sensibilities twenty years later: the use of lighting contributes to thematic ambience and suggests the "moods" of particular characters; the deployment of landscape works in the service of dramatic meaning; and the manipulation of composition, camera movement, montage, and gesture suggest "expressive force."[21]

As a veteran of Hollywood filmmaking, Ford was also influenced by *that* history of picturing Mexico and Mexicans. Gallagher comments on Ford's "iconic" abstractions—"*a* fugitive, *an* Indian woman, *a* lieutenant of police"—but does not link them to the particularities from which each generality is extricated.[22] Del Río is not merely "*an* Indian woman." She represents Ford's, Hollywood's, and America's perception of a Mexican Indian woman. And this Mexican Indian woman is placed in a "Mexico" that is an American version of Mexico.

In silent films, Mexico had functioned primarily as a backdrop, a mythic space of revolutionary fervor and revolution, populated by unsmiling groups of Indian peasants; swarthy, mustached *banditos*; and smiling, sexually available *señoritas*.[23] In later films, the Mexican Revolution, a civil war motivated by complex historical and political divisions, provided a different kind of ambience for Hollywood adventure stories, although Mexican stereotypes remained the same. Hollywood's Revolutionary Mexico appeared on screen as a place of anarchy, social unrest, and fanaticism.[24] However, while indebted to conventions of historical representations, *The Fugitive* also addressed contemporary concerns of the director and of the sociopolitical context in which it was produced.

Both Greene's novel and Ford's film took a "historiographical and anthropological role" in fashioning Mexico for a non-Mexican audience. Moreover, these personal imaginings transformed Mexico into a backdrop for writing a history and anthropology of the self in the same way that most colonialists placed themselves at the center of their colonial narratives. At the same time, Greene and Ford's fashionings of Mexico were not produced out of thin air. They were informed, on one hand, by existing colonial understandings of that nation and, on the other, by representations constructed by Mexico itself through various forms of cultural and industrial operations. In other words, I wish to remind readers of the ways in which Mexico participated in the reconstruction of its image in the twentieth century through cinema, art, and other commercial practices (such as tourism).

*Mexico functioned as a geographic and historical "back lot" for Hollywood in the 1930s and 1940s. Photograph courtesy of the Museum of Modern Art, New York.*

Although *The Fugitive* and *The Power and the Glory* did partake in a general mode of ethnography, at the same time they performed their ethnographies through different modes of narrativizing and representing. Gallagher argues that the screenplay adapted by Ford and Dudley Nichols needs to be considered as "a work in itself" rather than as a "staging of Greene's novel."[25] Contemporary scholars of adaptation concur with Gallagher's thesis of adaptation. Judith Mayne criticizes theories of film adaptation that posit the "novel as a source, the film as a 'faithful' or 'distorted,' 'adequate' or 'inadequate' rendition of it." She argues that this level of analysis is "ahistorical and limited only to the most isolated aesthetic concerns."[26] Rather, Mayne insists that we must consider how films and novels clarify the contradictions of culture and history through particular conventions of technology, mode of production, and genre. Under this rubric, *The Fugitive,* a product of the Hollywood system of narrative, representational, and industrial system and made in 1947, could therefore be considered as "a work in itself," as Gallagher alleges.

However, although it is important to differentiate the two texts on the basis of modes of practice, it is also necessary to theorize a relation *between* them. This relation is one of translation—specifically, a rerendering of Mexico into forms discernible to audiences for western movies. Translation is not merely a process of "rendering one language into another."[27] Writing and representing the other are "colonizing gestures," according to Tejaswini Niranjana.[28]

> Translation produces strategies of containment. By employing certain modes of representing the other—which it thereby also brings into being—translation reinforces hegemonic versions of the colonized, helping them acquire the status of what Edward Said calls representations, or objects without history.[29]

I would suggest, however, that history figures significantly in the production of representations of the colonized. It is not that other cultures are constructed outside of time or space; it is that the colonized acquire the status of objects without *their own* history. They are situated within a temporal and spatial framework that makes sense for the colonizer. In other words, they are figured as participants in *our* history, as players in the narrative flow that explains history and the world according to the colonizer's logic and understanding.

Throughout Hollywood's history, Mexico and Mexicans (as well as other cultural and ethnic groups) have served as objects without their own history. They have served as background material, simple peasants who wear colorful clothing and live in small but exotic villages. Or they have been foils for white heroes, in the form of "greasers," *banditos,* or beautiful but wily *señoritas.*

## Mexico in the Service of the United States

Like earlier films whose narratives played out in Mexican territory, *The Fugitive* made Mexico and Mexicans a backdrop for working out American cultural and political enigmas in the 1940s.[30] Although Ford changed or eliminated some of the particulars of Greene's novel, he preserved its fundamental proposals, including its decidedly pro-Catholic stance and its condemnation of communism. However, these proposals are situated within a personal and sociohistorical context different from Greene's, and it is within this context that we must situate possible meanings the film generated as well as the American public's response to the film.

Ward Bond's voice-over in the first scene informs the audience that the film was "entirely made in our neighboring republic, Mexico, at the kind invitation of the Mexican government and the Mexican motion picture industry." Bond's narration, however, proceeds to detach the film from its specific place. "Its locale is fictitious," he tells us. "It could be a small state one thousand miles to the north or south of the equator."

On one hand, this narration fits with America's understanding of Latin America as an undifferentiated region with a Spanish-speaking population. On the other hand, despite its initial disavowal, the story, the mise-en-scène, and the characters of *The Fugitive* explicitly locate the film in a Mexico that North American viewers had already experienced through Hollywood westerns and musicals, through Mexico's promotion of tourism in the 1930s and 1940s, and through popular literary and journalistic accounts of the recent history of the Mexican Revolution. *The Fugitive* thus participated in America's cultural production of a modern Mexico that was domesticated and immediately recognizable.[31]

The themes of Christianity and anticommunism are played out in the film against a spectacle that Americans had come to associate with Mexico: a barren yet exotic landscape, populated by poor, simple peasants and violent, barbarous revolutionaries. Although Greene's novel is explicit about the narrative's taking place in Mexico, Ford dispensed with details that identified the country. Yet the film's setting, the appearance of known Mexican actors such as del Río and Armendáriz, its use of Mexican stereotypes, and its focus on a civil war that is explicitly anticlerical could not disguise its location in the imaginations of U.S. audiences.

Greene's priest is a doubting Catholic as well as a drunkard and

*Del Río's María Dolores symbolizes religious faith in opposition to Armendáriz's fanatical and godless socialism in* The Fugitive. *Photograph courtesy of the Museum of Modern Art, New York.*

adulterer. He embodies both good and evil, as does the police lieutenant. In Ford's version, the priest, as the representative of the Church, is a doubting but essentially good man, whereas the lieutenant (Armendáriz), corrupted by his radical devotion to the ideology of the Revolution, represents the evils of communism. His moral and political depravity is symbolized by his elevation of political doctrine over human life at the social level and, on a personal level, by his refusal to acknowledge that he is the father of María Dolores's baby. (This is a significant change from the novel. In Greene's version, the priest is the child's father and the child is a young girl who occupies a significant place in the narrative.)

For Quentin Falk, this change is evidence of "the great director's inherent streak of sentimental Irish Catholicism," a streak that surfaces in *The Informer* (1935), *Mary of Scotland* (1936), and *The Plough and the Stars* 1936).[32] According to Ford and his cowriter, Dudley Nichols, however, the change was necessary in order to get the film past Hollywood censors. Nichols has noted that Greene's novel "was of a guilty priest and we could have no such guilty priest."[33] The film, then, according to the director and the screenwriter, became an allegory of the passion play, with Fonda's priest serving as the Christ figure, the mad beggar as Judas, and del Río as Mary Magdalene. Despite Ford's explanation, María Dolores's Catholicism and her motherly devotion to her child and chaste reverence for the priest also exemplify popular anticommunist sentiment; communism was viewed as a threat to U.S. familial and religious foundations.

Richard Slotkin argues that the U.S. public's response to the Mexican Revolution was activated "by fear of domestic radicalism," a fear grounded in racist attitudes fueled by eugenic discourses. He notes that the eugenic writer Eugene Stoddard saw the Mexican Revolution as "a key battle . . . in the 'rising tide of color.'"[34] Lacking the information and the drive to comprehend the complex historical, social, and political causes of Mexico's civil war, Americans could only read the Mexican Revolution in relation to their own attitudes and prejudices and to U.S. internal political relations in the second decade of the new century.[35]

When troops returned home from the European and Pacific fronts, the United States faced a decade of political, ideological, and sociological crises, none of which Hollywood escaped. Conservative politicians, religious leaders, and intellectuals had long regarded Hollywood as a hotbed of leftist political activity. In 1947, the same year Ford's film was released, the House Un-American Activities Committee (HUAC) convened to investigate the "Communist Infiltration of the Motion Picture Industry." HUAC targeted screenwriters and directors as perpetrators of the anti-American sentiment that conservative critics believed pervaded the movies.[36] Del Río herself was a victim of this witch-hunt. In 1954, U.S. customs denied her a visa to come to Hollywood to star in *The Broken Lance* on the basis of her association with "known communists." Katy Jurado, another Mexican actress working in Hollywood, took her place in the picture.[37]

A number of postwar film critics saw in *The Fugitive* an overtly anticommunist argument that successfully pitted democracy (in the form of freedom of religion) against communism (in the form of violent, antireligious actions). *Variety* called *The Fugitive* "a masterpiece of filmmaking. . . . A modern paraphrase of the passion play." *Variety*'s reviewer also drew a link between the film's depiction of the government's attempt to destroy the Catholic Church and communist antireligious ideology, writing that "as the Soviet government similarly tried to wipe out religion in Russia . . . *The Fugitive* will probably be widely regarded as an attack on Communism."[38]

Bosley Crowther of the *New York Times* read the film as a metaphor, "a terrifying struggle between strength and weakness in a man's soul . . .

a thundering modern parable on the indestructibility of faith, a tense and significant conflict between freedom and brute authority."[39] The reviewer for the *New Republic,* on the other hand, resented the explicit religious symbolism that pervaded Ford's film and complained that "the film was made to the propaganda standards of professional Catholicism."[40] Similarly, John McCarthy of the *New Yorker* complained that "the film takes for granted that anyone connected with the Church is good and that anyone connected with the State is bad."[41]

RKO aggressively exploited both the religious and the political agendas of the film. As part of its promotional strategy, the studio mailed a letter and descriptive folder to more than two hundred thousand Catholic priests, Catholic schools, and Protestant ministers in the United States. Fourteen thousand similar mailings were sent to various women's clubs that discussed moving pictures and their effects on the moral climate of the nation. RKO's efforts were successful. *The Fugitive* was officially recognized by the Catholic Church and presented with an award from *Signs,* a nationally distributed Catholic magazine.

While appealing to U.S. political and spiritual concerns, del Río's Mary Magdalene also fit within Mexican cinema's understandings of Mexican femininity. Just as Ford borrowed aesthetic ideas from Fernández and Figueroa, he also borrowed certain representational strategies. For example, as in Fernández's *María Candelaria,* del Río's María Dolores visually and symbolically represents the classical Mexican cinematic virgin/whore figure. We are made aware of this function in her initial scene. The priest arrives at the door of a church, enters, and kneels down to cross himself and pray. As he dips his hand into the basin of holy water, the camera tilts up to reveal del Río watching him. Dressed in white, she stands bathed in a pool of light, holding her baby, an obvious reference to the Virgin Mary holding the Christ child. In a close-up, her face framed by her white rebozo, she asks, "Who are you? Why are you here? I know all the men in the village. Are you a thief or a murderer?" In this scene María Dolores represents both whore (she "knows" all the men in the village) and virgin. While the film constantly reminds the audience that she had her baby out of wedlock, María Dolores is at the same time presented as a profoundly faithful Catholic who is willing to sacrifice herself to save the priest.

Borrowing from stereotypes in Mexican cinema, *The Fugitive* translated del Río into a specifically American understanding of Mexican femininity in order to make her character comprehensible to an American public. This translation was realized through conventional Hollywood representations of gendered and racialized national identities, which were then situated within a narrative structure that was familiar to American audiences. At the same time, this translation also borrowed from Mexican cinema's own production of Indian femininity. That is, Hollywood's production of the Mexican woman relied on existing representations found in the films and popular culture of Mexico that circulated globally.

As discussed earlier, in *María Candelaria* Mexico's virgin/whore archetype was the official symbol of Mexican female national identity. In the Mexican film, women are metaphorically and visually aligned with nature and spirituality, whereas men stand in for society and the profane. Men are worldly and thus sinful; women are victims and therefore sinless. *The Fugitive* recapitulates this opposition. Although Ford's treatment of women is often described as reproducing the virgin/whore dichotomy, in regard to this particular film one needs to consider not only the generic oppositions found in his Hollywood westerns but also his familiarity with and admiration of Fernández's work in Mexican cinema and Fernández's participation in the making of *The Fugitive*.

Ford's depiction of Mexicans as Indians is also indebted to both Hollywood's and Mexican cinema's representations. As discussed in chapter 1, Hollywood's earliest rendition of Mexicanness was the character of the "greaser," a dark-skinned, Indian-looking peasant. As I showed in chapter 4, beginning with *Redes* and *Janitzio*, Mexican cinema's nationalist project developed a particular cinematic figure of the Mexican Indian, a figure influenced by the nationalistic art of Rivera and other muralists. Their paintings reinforced stereotypical representations of racial and ethnic divisions that marked Mexican society since the Spanish conquistadors first mated with Indian women in the fifteenth century. Indians in this "national art" were portrayed as pure and simple, like children who had to be led to social (and revolutionary) consciousness) by the intellectual mestizo elite. The "Indianist" films of the Golden Age reproduced these stereotypes.

*Janitzio* narrates the story of a young Indian girl, Eréndia, who becomes the mistress of a white engineer in order to save her fiancé and who is subsequently stoned to death by the villagers for violating local sexual taboos. The film updates Mexico's myth of the origin of the Mexican race, the La Malinche/Cortés union, the first interracial romance in Mexican myth and history that produced a multiracial son. In *Janitzio,* an Indian woman is punished for the sins of the white male.

*Redes* is about a group of poor Indian fishermen who go on strike against a greedy criollo agent.[42] One of the directors, Fred Zinnemann, has written that "it was hoped that films [such as *Redes*] might help to extend their awareness of each other as compatriots sharing the same human problems."[43] However, according to Mexican critic Carlos Monsiváis, despite the noble intentions of the state and the filmmakers, rather than interrogating the social causes of the Indians' marginal status, *Redes* glorifies their stoic acceptance of poverty.[44]

*The Fugitive* reconsiders these earlier filmic national images of racial difference. The police lieutenant reminds a group of Indians who are waiting to be tried for "drunk and disorderly conduct," "I am an Indian just like you." However, the film goes out of its way to paint him in a different light by situating him as a member of a different class, educated, a socialist whose moral code is in the service of the state, and fiercely antireligious. The Indians, conversely, are uneducated, nonpartisan, profoundly moral, and profoundly Catholic.

According to Edward Said, colonial modes of translation in literary and scientific writing about the Orient in the nineteenth century assumed the forms of "regulatory codes, classifications, specimen cases, periodical reviews, dictionaries, grammars, commentaries, editions, translations."[45] The knowledges produced by these scientific practices were translated into popular discourse by nineteenth-century literary "pilgrims" (such as Gustave Flaubert, François-Auguste-René de Chateaubriand, Benjamin Disraeli, and Sir Richard Burton). The recounting of individual pilgrimages to the Orient situated the pilgrim/author at the center of the narrative. Although "every pilgrim sees things his own way," this seeing is shaped and limited by already existing literary and scientific translations of that culture.[46] Twentieth-century writers adopted these practices of knowledge production and translation. In addition, new modes, such as the cinema, appropriated and transformed these knowledges through technologically specific conventions.[47]

The process of adaptation, of converting a text from one form (a novel) into another (a film), involves commentary and transformation, which are both functions of translation. *The Fugitive* is a complex, multilayered text that retranslates Greene's interpretation of Mexico through Hollywood's narrative, representational, and industrial practices; through the ideological framework of postwar America; and through a lens of individual subjectivity. In turn, del Río is an equally complex amalgamation of Mexican and U.S. discursive and imagistic productions of Mexican femininity.

Each phase of the translation process (from Mexico to diary to novel to movie and from Mexican woman to Mexican cinematic woman to Hollywood Mexican woman) was in turn grounded within the context of postcolonialist writing practices. In these practices, the colonialist (or neocolonialist) constructed representations and modes of representations of the postcolonial subject. In the case of postcolonial relations, translation is not merely an "interlingual process"; it is a "problematic," or a complex of practices that entails reading, interpretation, disruption, and supplementation. This problematic "authorizes and is authorized by certain classical notions of representation and reality" that are informed by histories of colonialism and relations of power that ensue from those histories.[48]

It is this problematic that links *The Power and the Glory* to *The Fugitive* and that requires a critical analysis of the relation between the "source" and the "rendition." It is the same problematic that forces us to examine Hollywood's understanding of the relation between its cinematic vision of Mexico and the nation-state called Mexico and between the character of María Dolores and Dolores del Río as Mexican woman.

# 6

# Race on the Range

After two successful decades in Mexican cinema and theater, del Río returned to Hollywood in the 1960s to star as an Indian woman in two westerns: *Flaming Star* (1960, Don Siegel), with Elvis Presley, and John Ford's *Cheyenne Autumn* (1964).[1] Outside of a few appearances on American television, del Río had been out of American public life for more than a decade, and she was no longer considered a Hollywood movie star. Obviously, she did not enjoy the same kind of celebrity she had savored thirty years earlier.[2] Close to sixty when she portrayed the Indian squaw Neddy Barton in *Flaming Star*, del Río was no longer the "most perfect feminine figure in Hollywood"; she was an older woman.

The "older" woman occupied (and occupies) a different place in Hollywood's understanding of femininity. Hollywood has historically differentiated categories of femininity based on age. In films of the 1930s and 1940s, the older woman was primarily asexual: she was a mother, a grandmother, or a maid. If her sexuality was at all acknowledged, it was labeled "perverse" in the form of prostitution, rape, or debased desire for a younger man. From the 1950s on, the aging woman faced increased pressures due to the commodification of female sexual allure, an allure that was specifically linked to youthfulness.[3] Even today, when science and medical prac-

*An elderly del Río returns to Hollywood to star as an Indian woman in Ford's* Cheyenne Autumn. *Sal Mineo plays her son in the film. Photograph courtesy of the Museum of Modern Art, New York.*

tices promote drugs and procedures that propose to "stop" or "reverse" the aging process, successful white actresses like Meryl Streep and Susan Sarandon bemoan the fact that they are offered only "certain kinds" of roles: mothers, nuns, or, occasionally, the "older woman" who is the object of a younger man's attention. In these films, the older woman's sexuality is coded as aggressive, insatiable; she is a "fatal attraction." Sexual relations are articulated as erotically charged struggles for power between males and defeminized women.

In her earlier films, del Río's roles—as a half-breed Indian, a Mexican *señorita,* a Gypsy, or a Polynesian princess—were inflected by a star text that accentuated her youthful sexuality as "exotic," "aristocratic," and therefore desirable. Her sexuality was overdetermined; she was "oversexed." No longer a star in the 1960s, del Río is depersonified. She disappears into the narrative and formal conventions of her films. In *Flaming Star* and *Cheyenne Autumn,* it is the genre that is oversexed. Del Río becomes part of the structure of that genre; she is generic, functioning as a *cipher* of sexuality.

Although del Río no longer commanded the same kind of onscreen attention, desire, or identification as the exotic Luana in *Bird of Paradise,* the "sweet and naive" Dove in *Girl of the Rio,* or the aristocratic Belinha in *Flying Down to Rio* had, the aging Mexican star still served the same narrative function she had in the 1920s and 1930s. Her presence as a "nonwhite woman-structure" signified a narrative disruption, an enigma that had to be resolved before the film's plot could come to its logical conclusion.[4]

## Race and the Western Genre

The notion of race and racial difference occupied a different place in the postwar American imagination and in social and economic practice than it had in the 1920s and 1930s. By the 1960s, race had become a central issue in political and cultural discourse. The U.S. Supreme Court outlawed school segregation and, in 1967, declared state antimiscegenation laws unconstitutional. Americans took part in, or witnessed on television, the Montgomery bus boycott and interracial violence, and black culture infiltrated white culture in northern urban neighborhoods, in schools, and in popular music.[5] Scientific racism had been officially replaced by what Peggy Pascoe terms a "modernist racial ideology," a set of racial discourses that promoted "color-blindness" while disavowing any inherent link between biology and race.[6]

Although these notions and social practices did influence filmic constructions and readings of racialized sexuality in the Hollywood western in the 1960s, it would be naive to argue that *Flaming Star* and *Cheyenne Autumn* merely reflected contemporary racial discourse. Both films did respond to sociocultural pressures around questions of race and gender in the 1960s, but they also retained many of the conservative and mythical elements of the classical Hollywood western. Thus, for example, both films evidence the genre's preoccupation with masculinity and women's service in the advancement of that masculinity. And both films retain the western narrative opposition that equates whites with civilization and Native Americans with savagery. Specifically, *Cheyenne Autumn* and *Flaming Star* both go out of their way to insist that whites and Native Americans *are* different and that *that* fundamental problem is the real barrier to the melting-pot theory of American national identity.[7]

Based on a popular novel by Clair Huffaker, *Flaming Star* is a story that places race at the center of its narrative. A Kiowa uprising on the Texas frontier finds a young half-breed, Pacer (Presley), in the center of a race war in nineteenth-century America. Twenty years earlier, Pacer's father, Sam Burton, purchased a young squaw named Neddy (del Río) from her

*Del Río and Elvis Presley as mother and son in* Flaming Star. *Photograph courtesy of the Museum of Modern Art, New York.*

father for a rifle and a half bag of gunpowder. Burton brought Neddy home to help take care of his son from a previous marriage. This marriage of convenience grew into one of love. They had another son and worked their land for twenty years, enjoying neighborly, if restrained, relations with other frontier families who lived near them. When the local Kiowas wage war on the white settlers who have pushed them farther and farther out of their homelands, the Burtons' neighbors turn against them and they are forced to confront the miscegenational basis of their familial structure. The central conflict in the film emerges as a struggle between the white community and the racially tainted Burton family.

*Cheyenne Autumn,* Ford's final western, tells the story of a tribe of Cheyenne Indians who attempted a grueling 1,500-mile journey from an Oklahoma reservation to their homeland on the Yellowstone River in 1878. The three-hour epic, shot in 70mm Panavision, stars del Río in the role of an English-speaking "Spanish Woman" who is married to one of the chief's sons. The other major Indian roles are played by the Mexican actors Gilbert Roland and Ricardo Montalban and by Italian American actor Sal Mineo.[8]

Ford's film approaches the race question from the point of view of an aging army officer (Richard Widmark) who participates in the U.S.

government's effort to prevent the Indians from completing their odyssey. The narrative is presented in the form of a personal story of coming to terms with racism. This moral reformation in the hero is facilitated through the intervention of a woman, a Quaker schoolteacher (Carroll Baker), with whom Widmark's character is in love.

From the dime novels of the nineteenth century through contemporary films such as *Unforgiven* (1992) and *Dances with Wolves* (1990), the idea of a white national identity necessarily included nonwhites. This idea was not very far removed from the experiences of frontier settlers. As white Americans moved west and encountered Native Americans and Mexicans, they also confronted sexual and marriage practices that contradicted their own moral beliefs and legal customs. John D'Emilio and Estelle B. Freedman insist that "the interplay of racial and sexual ideology can be seen clearly in the attitudes" of white settlers of the western frontier. The image of the dark-skinned Indian as immoral and sexually perverse laid the groundwork for the pioneers' encounter with Mexicans as they traveled farther west into the northern territories of Mexico (territories that eventually became New Mexico and California).[9] Cronon, Miles, and Gitlin point out that throughout the history of westward expansion and encounter, "sexual fantasy thus helped enforce the boundary between 'savage' and 'civil' society in ways that amplified frontier hostilities."[10] Del Río's presence in *Flaming Star* and *Cheyenne Autumn* exemplifies how this erotic fantasy became central to cinematic accounts of westward expansion. In order to understand precisely how a figure like del Río functioned in the western—in order to *see* the disappearing act, in other words—we need to understand the institutionalization, organization, and mechanism of the form itself.

The western film genre participated in the production and circulation of one of the foundational narratives of American national identity: the "frontier myth." In a thesis articulated by the historian Frederick Jackson Turner, the western moment—the middle of the nineteenth century—is constituted as an "epic moment" in American history and is defined by its setting (the western frontier), its set of characters, and the kinds of stories it narrates. Turner has been rightly criticized for his univocal "model of a universal frontier process that was everywhere and always the same."[11]

However, following Turner, historians have argued that the European colonist was made into an American as a result of "his" encounter with the frontier (the pioneer of history and popular culture was, until recently, always male).[12] This frontier was a geographic space defined by landscapes and national borders as well as a social space delimited by race, gender, class, and ancestry. The frontier was primarily a place that was "uncivilized" and not white.[13]

Alongside the advancement of this scholarly explanation of the "frontier process," there developed a popular understanding of the West. Ann Fabian notes that scholars who attended the American Historical Association annual conference in Chicago in 1893 would have had a chance to experience "a version of the western past every bit as compelling as Turner's": Buffalo Bill Cody's Wild West Show.[14] Outside the walls of the academic conference, the American public was not only enjoying Buffalo Bill, but was reading western dime novels and listening to popular western music.[15] These popular versions of the frontier thesis were imbued with a nostalgia for a mythic rural past that was less complicated and morally superior to contemporary industrial life.

Significantly, audiences of wild west shows, readers of western romances, and, later, postwar audiences of Hollywood film westerns recalled a national history that consecrated, justified, and idealized America's conquest of Native American and Mexican territory.[16] While popular narratives of westward expansion and nation building played out upon the mythical space of the western frontier, the terrain of racial difference and race mixing was the interior, or unconscious, domain within which narrative conflict was dramatized. According to popular history, the new American was shaped as much by the development of a particularly American racial discourse and set of practices as "he" was by his encounter with the wilderness. Turner, the academic historian, agreed. He wrote that Europe's "invasion . . . and the resistance to it by the continent's existing inhabitants—[is] the pivotal event in American history."[17]

Novelists and filmmakers capitalized on the dramatic potential of the oppositional theme of the frontier story.[18] In their writings and films, the western myth emerged as a myth of a particular antagonistic relation between white Europeans and Native Americans that took on a specific racial cast: the white settler represented "civilization" and the barbarous and uncivilized Native American stood in for "nature" in novels and film. Whites were moral and right because they were white; Indians were immoral and heathen because they were not white. Race relations on the frontier were actually much more complex, marked by regional, economic, and ideological differences.[19] Patricia Nelson Limerick notes that American territorial "expansion involved peoples of every background: English, Irish, Cornish, Scottish, French, German, Portuguese, Scandinavian, Greek, and Russian," not to mention the diverse Indian, Hispanic, and Asian populations that moved across the frontier.[20]

Although western films owe many of their premises, icons, stories, spaces, and conventions to earlier forms of the western genre, the cinema developed a particularly cinematic vision of the American frontier. Although some early western films did offer seemingly sympathetic portrayals of Indians as "noble savages," most treated Indians as impediments to American geographic expansion. William S. Hart, a filmmaker and western star, made a number of racist silent westerns and was influential in the development of the film genre.[21] In *Hell's Hinges* (1916), one of the evil characters, Silk Miller, is defined by the script as having "the oily craftiness of the Mexican." Miller corrupts the good Reverend Robert Henley, who succumbs to the seduction of a half-breed prostitute. The "moral weakness of the minister is equated with his racially indiscriminate passions."[22] The "half-breed" is the primary enemy of American geographic and social expansion in other early western films, such as *The Aryan* (1916), *Closin' In* (1918), and *The Flaming Forest* (1926). Richard Slotkin points to Hart's influence on the western film genre, writing that the filmmaker "brought to the movies a clear and well-established vision of the West as region and Western as story form."[23] According to Slotkin, Hart was influenced by James Fenimore Cooper's western romances, in which "sexual passion is seen as the most fundamental expression of racial consciousness or instinct, and the characteristic of the true Anglo-Saxon is represented as an intense exclusivity in preferring women of his own race, the purer the better."[24] Like Cooper's novels, Hollywood westerns have always manifested a "persistent obsession with masculinity" and with "the problem of becoming a man."[25] However, as del Río's presence demonstrates, women and race figure prominently in the genre's masculine narratives. She is the "trouble in the text." In *Flaming Star* she is the Indian woman married to the white man, a generic inconsistency. And in *Cheyenne Autumn* she is a sympathetic Indian (sympathetic because she is a woman) and a voice of reason, two other contradictions to western generic conventions.

The classical western is obsessed with race, racialized sexuality, and interracial romance. Indians, both male and female, are coded as "oversexed": white men cannot resist the allure or the availability of Indian women, and Indian warriors are obsessed with raping white women. The problem of racialized sexuality is played out among three major characters: the white male hero, the white woman who redeems the hero, and the figure of the other—the Mexican, Indian, or half-breed. The racial other menaces white womanhood through kidnap and rape and challenges white males through armed combat and threats to white male sovereignty.

In its 1960s sensibility, *Flaming Star* inverted the conventional western formula by making a half-breed the hero, situating an Indian woman as a victim, and positioning white men in the role of villains. *Cheyenne Autumn* similarly encouraged sympathy for Indians while castigating whites for moral corruption and for allegiance to law and authority instead of ethical standards. At the time the films were released, critics saw both as liberal attempts to respond to the western's historical portrayal of Indians. For some critics, the films countered the long and brutal history of the western genre, in which the Indian had functioned as the major enemy of white America and the major impediment to national development in the nineteenth century. The *Hollywood Reporter* described *Flaming Star* as "an oblique and sometimes moving plea for racial tolerance." The MPAA reviewer found the film to be a "sympathetic portrayal of race by Dolores and Elvis."[26]

Bosley Crowther, writing in the *New York Times,* called *Cheyenne Autumn* "a beautiful and powerful motion picture that stunningly combines a profound and passionate story of mistreatment of American Indians with some of the most magnificent and energetic cavalry-and-Indian lore ever put upon the screen."[27] Other reviewers, while acknowledging Ford's attempt, viewed the result as a failure. The reviewer for *Time* accused Ford of "dehydrating history," saying that when the Cheyennes "are not struggling with the white man's words, they address one another in Navajo."[28] Brendan Gill risked movie fans' ire when he said that *Cheyenne Autumn* "is far and away the most boring picture of 1964."[29] And Stanley Kauffmann offered the most brutal commentary: "We are supposed to have sympathy for [the Cheyenne] by the facts of their underdog situation; and we are to know the good guys from the bad guys by this sympathy. The white men who kill or harry Indians most reluctantly are the best."[30]

Contemporary historians argue that both films are not really "Indian" stories at all but are about black-and-white relations in the United States in the 1960s. These critics contextualize the films in relation to questions that were being brought to the forefront of American life by the civil rights movement. Richard Slotkin, for example, asserts that during the 1960s, Native Americans were "pressed into service as symbols in political and cultural controversies that chiefly concerned non-Indian groups."[31] Michael Coyne labels *Cheyenne Autumn* a "'Civil Rights' Western that recasts the dispossessed Cheyenne trekking back to their Dakota homeland as nineteenth-century Freedom Marchers."[32]

One can speculate that some filmmakers may have employed the western genre to talk about contemporary race problems, or that certain films may have been part of a carefully crafted approach to deal with racial tensions.[33] However, such an insistence on reading these films "in context" limits our understanding of how race and history have conjoined in U.S. culture across specific historical eras. On the one hand, race became a generic category *apart from* specific identifiable characteristics of various races in the western. The definitions of race exceeded their limits, and all that is needed now is the *idea of race,* or race in the abstract: it is the opposition between white and nonwhite that matters, not the particular biological differences. And in films like *Flaming Star* and *Cheyenne Autumn,* racially coded stars such as del Río, Sal Mineo, Ricardo Montalban, and Gilbert Roland authenticate the otherness of racial difference.

On the other hand, it is crucial to recognize that our understanding of the Native American's role in U.S. history has been part of our national folklore for almost two hundred years.[34] This understanding operates under the rubric of a "common sense history [that] reflects and refracts images from the past and the present," in the words of Marcia Landy.[35] Thus, although both *Flaming Star* and *Cheyenne Autumn* could be seen as allegories of contemporary racial tensions, in the collective unconscious of American audiences neither of the narratives can be divorced from America's memory of that other history of our initial encounter with the "savage" red man and red woman.

At the same time, stories about the formation of American national identity are located in an "imagined" historical time and space. That is to say that although the Native American has appeared in oral, written, and photographic productions about our collective identity, the logic of racism in the nineteenth century operated very differently from that of the twentieth century. Moreover, it is impossible to remember (and thus to understand in the sense that Americans living in the nineteenth century understood) what it "felt" like to be a white man participating in the construction of a new nation and a new nationalism. Thus neither those westerns that promoted anti-Indian racism nor those that criticized it could ever really get at the structures of those relations; they could only be imagined within the structures of racism in the twentieth century.

Unlike people, nations "have no clearly identifiable births. . . . the nation's biography can not be written evangelically," but must be fashioned forward, toward the moment in which the narrative "takes place."[36] The imagined memory of the origination and evolution of the American nation had to be constructed as a continual process that was moral, foreordained, and invested with a future. If some twentieth-century revisionist narratives acknowledged the white settlers' participation in genocide, it was explained as a practice that could not be avoided: it was kill or be killed.

## Nation, Desire, and the Western Genre

The history of the identity of the United States as a nation is linked to the ambiguous concept of the melting pot. On the one hand, the notion of a "natural" fusion of cultures and races attempted to acknowledge that the United States was a nation of immigrants. On the other hand, popular and public discourse historically insisted on the preeminence of a white, Anglo-Saxon heredity in the face of interbreeding and the threat of racial degeneration. Although any form of racial intermarrying was seen as a threat to the purity of the white race in early films, a hierarchy of racial classification placed Indians as the greatest threat, southern Europeans as the least, and Asians and Mexicans "somewhere near the middle of the hierarchy" (African Americans did not figure at all in this hierarchy of possibility).[37]

Miscegenation is a central theme in the western film. Nonwhite women are generally not eligible for marriage to white heroes. Although Indian and Mexican women are often sympathetic characters, desirable, beautiful, submissive, and self-sacrificing, they nevertheless are doomed to death or some other form of narrative displacement in order to solve the potential problem of racial contamination.[38]

As in most classical Hollywood melodramas, desire is almost always a masculine prerogative in the western. However, women occupy a central, if unacknowledged, place in the historical myth of the West. In the western film, the white woman is a symbol of civilization in the garb of the school-teacher or the embodiment of legitimate or illegitimate sexuality in the role of the pioneer mother or the dance-hall prostitute. As the third element in the relation between the white hero and the racialized savage, she represents "the sexual fascination and fear associated with the rape of white women by savages."[39] She is also, most obviously, the reproducer of the white American race.

The Indian woman performs a similar function in westerns as do non-white women characters in other Hollywood genres: she is both desirable and forbidden, and that proscription makes her eminently more desirable. Sometimes she embodies the "eighteenth-century conception of the help-ful Pochahontas." At other moments she assumes the nineteenth-century "image of the savage and promiscuous squaw" who is indiscriminately available for any white man who wants her.[40] Like Luana in *Bird of Paradise,* the Indian squaw symbolizes the feminized other, dominated not merely by a the white man's physical strength, but also by his sexual potency.

In fact, both *Flaming Star* and *Cheyenne Autumn* position women—Indian and white—as the moral consciences of their cultures. If the western is fundamentally a male-directed narrative, it is also, in the words of Richard Dyer, "woman-inspired."[41] In *Flaming Star,* it is Neddy (and the male character Buffalo Horn, who is feminized as a man of peace and not a warrior) who appeals to her people to call off their war against the white settlement, and it is Roz (Barbara Eden), the white object of male desire, who challenges the racist beliefs and practices of the white community. Likewise, in *Cheyenne Autumn* Carroll Baker and the "Spanish Woman" join forces to try to persuade their men to stop killing each other.

*Cheyenne Autumn*'s and *Flaming Star*'s liberal melodramas of race relations were not novel.[42] Following the course of change in national politics and ideologies after World War II, Hollywood's genres were revised to address emerging concerns about America's perception of race. Postwar "social consciousness" films such as *Pinky* (1949, Elia Kazan), *Home of the Brave* (1949, Mark Robson), and *Intruder in the Dust* (1949, Clarence Brown) featured race as central to their narratives.

The western was an enduring and popular genre whose narrative conventions made it available for discussions of contemporary race relations. Between 1960 and 1969, approximately two hundred western feature films were released. Additionally, although the television western had declined from its peak in the late 1950s, long-running shows such as *Gunsmoke, Have Gun Will Travel, Maverick,* and *Wagon Train* were still broadcast weekly by the major networks.[43] Popular Italian-produced "spaghetti westerns," such as Sergio Leone's *A Fistful of Dollars* (1964) and *The Good, the Bad, and the Ugly* (1967) added to the currency of the genre's popularity. Thus, although the western of the 1960s may not have enjoyed the genre's former measure of popularity, westerns did continue to provide the American imagination with nostalgic, allegorical narratives of a shared national past. A number of films, such as *Broken Arrow* (1950, Delmer Daves) and *The Searchers* (1956, Ford) reexamined the industry's treatment of Indians and the question of miscegenation.

*Broken Arrow* is told from the point of view of a white prospector, Tom Jeffords (James Stewart). Jeffords's anti-Indian racism is transformed by two narrative elements: a wounded Apache boy he has rescued later saves him from death at the hands of a young Geronimo, and he falls in love with and marries an Indian woman. In both cases, the Indians' savagery is subdued: the boy's through his sacrifice for the white man, the woman's through sexual vanquishment. According to Slotkin, *Broken Arrow* "permitted the audience to indulge, and congratulate itself, on a 'liberal' attitude toward non-Whites without having to abandon the fundamental assurance of their own superiority."[44] *Cheyenne Autumn* proposes the same solution.

After documenting the Cheyenne's long, arduous journey, during which time the tribe faces hunger, bad weather, and white treachery, the standoff between the Indians and the army is finally resolved. However, the resolution comes about not through the tribe's fortitude or because of the dedication and heroism of the Indian chiefs, but through the last-minute intervention of the U.S. secretary of the interior (Edward G. Robinson), whose hero is Abraham Lincoln. In the words of John Cawelti, the mythical western setting and the conventional role of various characters in *Cheyenne Autumn* function as

> an artistic device for [violently] resolving problems rather than confronting their irreconcilable ambiguities. . . . In other words, the Indian rarely stands for a possible alternative way of life which implies a serious criticism of American society. Instead he poses a problem for the hero.[45]

Like *Flaming Star, The Searchers* is first and foremost a film about racial contamination. Ethan Edwards (John Wayne), a Confederate soldier who has never accepted the South's defeat, arrives at his brother Aaron's home in Texas after years of wandering and fighting. Secretly in love with Aaron's wife, Martha, Ethan plays the role of a wayward uncle to Martha's two daughters, Lucy and Debbie (Natalie Wood), while rejecting her adopted half-breed son, Martin (Jeffrey Hunter). While Ethan and Martin are off with an Indian scouting party, Comanches attack and kill Aaron, Martha, and Lucy and kidnap Debbie. The remainder of the film follows Ethan and Martin's search for Debbie over a period of more than five years.

Ethan intends to kill Debbie when he finds her, believing that she has been racially contaminated. As in the "imperial adventure film" or the "captivity narrative," it is the white male's fear of a sexual assault on his property, the white woman, that impels him to embark on the rescue adventure.[46] Earlier, I discussed Hollywood's positioning of woman as a commodity. Shohat and Stam show how the "rape and rescue trope . . . forms a crucial site in the battle over representation" in which both white and nonwhite women must be saved from the "dark rapist . . . polygamous Arabs, libidinous Blacks, and macho Latinos."[47] However, the metaphoric rape renders the commodity unusable; the woman has been "blackened" or cheapened by sexual defilement.

In *The Searchers,* racism is conquered through a number of narrative strategies. Debbie returns to the family, ostensibly unharmed. Ethan comes to see the Indian as human. Martin will marry a Swedish white girl, Laurie Jorgensen (Vera Miles), and their offspring will be whitened. This union promotes an acceptable interracial marriage. Martin is male and thus recuperable into national, white culture. He is only part Indian, and he has been "civilized"—raised by a white mother figure in a white household. His children will be whitened by Laurie's blood. Conversely, Debbie is not allowed to remain with the Indians and reproduce children whose blood will be diffused. The film does not explain why or how the offspring of Ethan's mixed marriage would be "white" whereas Debbie's children through Scar would be "Indian." It is an enigma that even liberalism cannot solve.

A similar logic drives the narrative of *Flaming Star*. Although the film treats Sam and Neddy's marriage with reverence, Pacer is not permitted to follow in his father's footsteps; the narrative does not allow him to "contaminate" the bloodline further by marrying a white girl. His brother, the full-blooded white man, gets the girl instead. Like many liberal westerns, *Flaming Star* proposes that two people of different races can love each other, but it admits that this relationship is not viable given the context of American racism. In other words, the film acknowledges the social basis of racism but refuses to offer a strategy for change. Moreover, like *Bird of Paradise*, Siegel's film suggests that even savage cultures won't permit interbreeding. Neddy tells her half-breed son that the Kiowas have rejected her as "the thin woman who deserted her own people" and describe her as "neither Kiowa nor white but filthy."

Initially, *Flaming Star* sets itself up as a classic western. The title sequence celebrates the western landscape with a series of wide shots depicting two men on horseback riding across the deserted Texas frontier. The opening scene takes place in the other space of the western, the home, a place that Laura Mulvey describes as the "signifier of stable space, the sphere of the family."[48] Sam and Neddy and their two sons, Clint and Pacer, are celebrating Clint's birthday with some neighbors. Neddy stands by the hearth, occupying the traditional space of the frontier mother.

This spectacle clearly intends to reference John Ford's westerns. The scene incorporates all the requisite Ford ingredients: the nuclear pioneer family, the white-and-blue Wedgewood china decorating the wooden table of a two-room frontier house that marks the European ancestry of the pioneer, and the celebration of this pioneer family through song and dance. However, the scene does not pay homage. Instead, *Flaming Star* advances an attack on the ideology of Ford's films, his veneration of the families who settled the frontier, his ideology of redemptive Christianity, and his

*Don Siegel's homage to John Ford's westerns:* Flaming Star. *Photograph courtesy of the Museum of Modern Art, New York.*

portrayal of Native Americans. Unlike Ford's western family, the mother in this film is a full-blooded Kiowa Indian and her son is a half-breed.

In the midst of this familial and communal celebration, one of the guests comments that Neddy's cooking is so good, you'd never know it was done by someone who was not "one of them." *Flaming Star* thus appears to acknowledge the core of racism that underlined the codification of U.S. national identity during the settlement of the West. At the same time, while the film promotes and celebrates intermarriage between two people of different races and suggests that race is not a valid category of difference, it condemns interbreeding for social and pragmatic reasons.

While *Cheyenne Autumn* does not confront the problem of miscegenation, it does propose the same "history" of the evolution of American national identity that *Flaming Star* does. Although Widmark's major is obviously Anglo-Saxon, most of the other characters are defined by stereotypical indicators of "ethnicity." Carroll Baker's Quaker teacher represents the contribution of the Nordic countries to the melting pot; Widmark's second in command is a kindly but dull-witted Pole; although the army's Irish doctor has a drinking problem, his religion makes him moral; and the commander of the army's northern outpost is a German immigrant

*"Whiteness" as American ethnic identity: Richard Widmark and Carroll Baker in* Cheyenne Autumn. *Photograph courtesy of the Museum of Modern Art, New York.*

who, although sympathetic to the plight of the Cheyenne, blindly believes that "authority must and will be obeyed," asking, "What will this world be without orders? Chaos? Anarchy?"

The narratives of *Flaming Star* and *Cheyenne Autumn* had to resolve the conflict between the plot's need for a "liberal" resolution to the race problem and a deeper compulsion to reaffirm the historically specific structuring element of racial difference. Both films mediate this narrative crisis through female characters. Both white and Indian women have to be returned to their "proper places" by patriarchal authority "so that order is restored to the world" of the western genre.[49]

In *Cheyenne Autumn*, the conventions of racial place are disturbed when Carroll Baker leaves the safety of the fort (one of the frontier spaces of whiteness) to accompany the Cheyenne on their journey. She confesses to her uncle, the Quaker pastor, that she believes "her place" is with the Indians. Throughout the difficult journey, she becomes more and more uncivilized and thus more and more sexualized: her clothes are dirty and torn, her hair is unkempt, her face and body are dirty, her emotions are out of control. The end of the film *rewhitens* her character, returning her to her "proper place" in the space and safety of whiteness.

*Flaming Star*'s resolution hinges on the restoration of the Indian woman and her half-breed son to their rightful place. *Flaming Star* must kill off Pacer and his mother in order for white national identity to be recuperated. The half-breed's body signifies what Mary Ann Doane calls an "*invisible* history." Doane writes that "the mulatto, as the sign of a historical miscegenation and a potential disabling of the polarization between

*Carroll Baker is "de-whitened" when she aligns herself with the Indians in* Cheyenne Autumn. *Photograph courtesy of the Museum of Modern Art, New York.*

black and white, is a particularly dangerous figure who requires extensive textual containment."⁵⁰ This figure of mixed blood confounds the notion of racial purity upon which the "imagined community" of the United States was founded.

At the moments of their deaths (Neddy is killed by a white man who is dying of wounds sustained in a Kiowa ambush; Pacer is mortally wounded by the Kiowas after he rescues his brother from the hands of a marauding Kiowa band), both renounce white civilization and return to the space of their heritage. After she sees the Kiowa's "flaming star" of death, Neddy crawls away from the Burton homestead and from her white husband to die alone on a hilltop above the house. Her hair, bound up and secured on top of her head for most of the film, falls wildly around her shoulders as she drags herself up the hill.

Pacer returns to town only to tell his brother that he has avenged their father's death. But he refuses to die as a white man, and he turns his horse and rides back to the wilderness. He, too, has seen the "flaming star." These narrative resolutions for the film's racial "problems" sustain the idea that racial difference is insurmountable. Despite the liberal thrust of the film's melting-pot ideology, the "laws of nature" must acknowledge the inherent difference and incompatibility between whites and Indians.

The film's liberal tendencies allow the audience to feel sorry for the Indians' demise. However, Siegel's film preserves the same fundamental laws of acceptable intermarriage the industry put forth in the 1930s in films like *Anna Christie*, as discussed in chapter 2. There are no more racial impediments to the joining of the two families. When Neddy and Pacer have been killed off, Clint's marriage to Roz, the acceptable white ethnic woman (her ancestry is Swedish) is subsequently guaranteed. With her blond hair, pale skin, and lithe figure, Roz represents whiteness; she is ultrawhite. As Doane describes the white woman in Hollywood films, "She is simply there, undisguised, *naturally* symbolic of all that the white men struggle to safeguard—white purity, white culture, whiteness itself."⁵¹

# Conclusion

*Racism does not, of course, move tidily and unchanged through time and history. It assumes new forms and articulates new antagonisms in different situations.*

Paul Gilroy, *There Ain't No Black in the Union Jack,* 1987

Dolores del Río provided an enigmatic fascination for Hollywood film-makers and film audiences for more than fifty years. Her racialized female body always, and necessarily, evoked anxieties about interracial sexual relations and miscegenation. In order to understand her "meaning" in films and in American culture, I have worked in the preceding chapters to clarify the links among what Richard Dyer has referred to as the "central relations between stars and specific instabilities, ambiguities and contradictions in the culture."[1] My purpose in this book has been to articulate the historically specific ways these relations were reproduced in del Río's star text and in in her films.

Throughout the writing of this book, I have to tried to think about the "meaning" of del Río in these seemingly inimical terms. On the one hand, del Río's star text aroused (and obtained) spectatorial desire among white audiences. On the other hand, her differences stimulated a collective uneasiness motivated by individual and public fears of racial contamination on the part of the dominant white majority. One could argue that the same set of antagonisms operates today in the cultural arena. How can this continued preoccupation be explained and disentangled from ahistorical explanations of race and racism? In this conclusion, I will argue that although

*Del Río as an "enigmatic fascination": publicity still from* What Price Glory.
*Photograph courtesy of the Museum of Modern Art, New York.*

every moment is certainly defined by its own set of discourses and practices, racial categories and racist discourses and practices continue to inform contemporary articulations of embodied difference.

Race has appropriated new bodies and definitions, and racism is
imagined and practiced in different ways in the United States at the end of
the twentieth century. In turn, the contemporary cinematic apparatus re-

veals itself through new structures of industrial organizations and practices; through revised forms of censorship, relations of production, distribution, and exhibition; in alternative sites of exhibition; through an elaborated convergence among movies, advertising, and consumer practices; and in the presence of and engagement with a different kind of subjectivity. At the same time, Hollywood continues to move ethnic and racially coded actors in and out of representations of racialized sexuality. Race still matters in the United States, and race and interracial romance are still viable commodities in Hollywood.

On the surface, current Hollywood films are more explicit about sex and race and about racialized sexuality. The industry *appears* to have renegotiated representations of racialized sexuality and interracial romance. Contemporary film audiences are participants in a complex and ambiguous cultural moment, marked on one hand by increased racial tension and racist rhetoric and on the other by a kind of "opening up" of the "race question" in the media.

In what some have described as a "boom," we have seen an unprecedented number of films directed by black, Asian American, and Hispanic filmmakers as well as the release of a substantial number of films featuring nonwhite actors in major character roles. Certain strategies of representing race relations, in fact, have become extremely profitable in the marketplace. Ed Guerrero has noted that since the 1980s, audiences have witnessed an increase in the number of black actors and actresses in Hollywood, not only in films directed by blacks, but also in "crossover" films, films made by white directors and marketed to a racially heterogeneous audience. He notes, however, that in terms of black and other nonwhite masculinities and femininities, "strategies of containment" continue to work at the level of sexuality.[2] Black males, for example, are generally perversely sexual (Eddie Murphy in *48 Hrs.*, 1982), or their sexuality is sublimated or ignored (Denzel Washington in *The Pelican Brief,* 1993). In films such as *48 Hrs.*, and the *Lethal Weapon* series, Danny Glover and Eddie Murphy are feminized, so to speak—put into what Guerrero terms the "protective custody" of the white characters, played by Nick Nolte and Mel Gibson, respectively.[3]

The pairing of two superstars, Julia Roberts and Denzel Washington, in *The Pelican Brief* was a calculated strategy designed to attract what Hollywood perceives to be racially and ethnically diverse audiences. However, although Roberts's and Washington's characters are narratively positioned to engage in a romantic affair, *The Pelican Brief* never follows through on that possibility. Prime-time television series such as *ER* and *Ally McBeal* promote and enact romance between black men and white women (as well as friendships among people of different races), while at the same time ignoring the issue of race. Race is thus both evident and absent.

Even in films like Spike Lee's *Jungle Fever* (1991), which has been heralded for challenging conventional representations of interracial sex, race remains a problematic and unsolvable enigma. Sharon Willis understands Lee's film as a "critical challenge to fantasies about race as *visible*."[4] Conversely, Guerrero finds that *Jungle Fever* "upholds every expectation and prohibition" related to interracial sexual relations that have been in place since the Hays Office Code and is no more oppositional than white Hollywood films.[5]

Although not yet as acclaimed as black filmmakers, Chicana/o directors are exhibiting a growing presence at the box office and are using their position to rethink Hispanic stereotypes.[6] According to Victor Fuentes, the Latina women in Chicano-directed films like *La Bamba, El Norte* (1983, Gregory Nava), and *Born in East L.A.* (1987, Cheech Marin) "are represented as hardworking women of moral strength and integrity. In spite of their physical beauty, there is very little emphasis on their sensuality."[7] Rosa Linda Fregoso, however, sees Latinas in *La Bamba* as "timeworn stereotypes . . . the object rather than the subject of the male gaze."[8] And although Fregosa commends *Born in East L.A.* for its "effective indictment of dominant official discourse," she criticizes the film's violent and thus "ambivalent treatment of women."[9]

My intention here is not to pit one critical reading against another. Rather, I wish to emphasize the difficulty of reading "race"—representations of race and racial tensions—as good or bad, right or wrong, positive or negative. I also want to problematize the reading of "readings of race" as dominant, oppositional, or negotiated. Willis's, Guerrero's, Fuentes's, and Fregoso's disparate readings are merely illustrative of the way in which all spectators, even we academics, are bound up in the tightly woven mesh of the historical moment. Their comments display the power of cinematic depictions of race to stimulate readings that are determined by political and personal situatedness and a felt need to develop critical strategies that oppose racism.

Hollywood films have *always* been racist because they are symptoms of a culture that has always been racist. Although some films have been more conspicuously racist than others, the racism of every Hollywood film has been informed by the social codes and discourses of the historical moment in which it was produced and by the narrative, generic, and aesthetic conventions of cinematic racial representations.

Thus, while del Río *always* represented an other woman, and while her otherness always signified "not white, not American," the implication of this otherness was linked to the instabilities, ambiguities, and contradictions of U.S. culture in a specific moment and place. Only through reading her star text in relation to those specificities can we understand what "otherness" could have meant to del Río's audiences.

This brings me to consider the position of "other" women in contemporary Hollywood. Although the most popular and successful female stars in the late 1990s are still white, a number of African American and Hispanic women have fashioned successful careers in Hollywood. Robin Givens, Whoopi Goldberg, Whitney Houston, Angela Bassett, Rosie Perez, Elizabeth Peña, Salma Hayek, and Jennifer Lopez command equitable fees and are offered more substantial roles than nonwhite actresses in the past. And, in some cases, their blackness, or brownness, while obvious, is rendered narratively and functionally invisible. I want to conclude by examining the political consequences of this annihilation.

Jennifer Lopez, a New York native of Puerto Rican descent, is one of the successful new ethnic stars. Beginning with supporting roles in *Money Train* (1995) and *Mi Familia* (1995), Lopez quickly moved into more substantial parts in *Jack* (1996), *Blood and Wine* (1997), *Anaconda* (1997), and *Selena* (1997). However, despite her varied roles and recent success, Lopez complains that "I'm still looked at as 'The Latina Actress.'" Indeed, a reviewer in my local newspaper, the *Raleigh News and Observer,* has written that "Lopez . . . has become Hollywood's fastest-rising starlet, in part because of her *exotic* bombshell looks. And in part, too, because the girl can act."[10]

Lopez declined to be interviewed about her role in *Selena* for an article on Latina actresses in the *Los Angeles Times.* According to that article, "It's not that Lopez doesn't want to be known as Latin—she hasn't changed her name or turned down the most high-profile Latin role in the biggest Latin-themed picture since *La Bamba.* It's that she and her managers don't want her to be limited by her ethnicity."[11] Understandably, many Latino and African American actors are looking to be recognized for their acting ability, not as racial or ethnic "types." According to *Selena*'s director, Gregory Nava, Elizabeth Peña "hates reading articles about Latinos in Hollywood, because it sounds like we're always bitching about the same damn thing. . . . Every time we project ourselves as a victim, the subliminal 'them' keeps us stuck in that place."[12]

Unlike del Río's career, which insisted on her ethnic and national otherness, the roles that Lopez and Peña are offered attempt to embody difference in a figure of hybridity. Lopez, for example, has appeared in a number of "nonethnic" roles in films like *Anaconda* and the 1998 adaptation of Elmore Leonard's novel *Out of Sight* (Steven Soderbergh). Unlike Lee's *Jungle Fever, Out of Sight* is not explicit about its presentation of interracial coupling. The comedic detective film stars Lopez in the role of Federal Agent Karen Cisco. In the film, Karen falls in love with Jack, a lovable but compulsive bank robber played by George Clooney.

In this film, discourses of liberal multiculturalism structure the narrative and inform the film's racial representations and configurations. *Out of Sight* seems to be a story about a world in which race doesn't matter. The film traverses the contested and racialized turf of criminality and the law in the United States: cops are white, black, and racially ambiguous; criminals are wealthy, heterosexual white males, gay Cubans off the streets of Miami, and tough blacks from the south side of Detroit; and a well-known white male star is romantically paired with an up-and-coming Latina star. Race is thus hypervisible yet discursively erased at the level of the narrative.

At this particular historical moment in the late twentieth century, American national identity, indeed the notion of the American "nation," is once again being hotly contested. The notion of hybridity is becoming less of an analytic term and more of a material reality. White birthrates are plummeting while African American and Hispanic births are on the rise. More and more people define themselves as being of "mixed" race. Although nonwhite groups make up the largest percentage of the lower socioeconomic strata and manifest higher infant mortality rates and shorter life spans, general demographic projections predict that within twenty years, whites will be the minority racial group in the United States.

Anti-immigration discourse and legislation have emerged in the 1990s in response to the influx of legal and illegal Spanish-speaking workers and the simultaneous and radical shift in regional demographics and culture. The inevitable battle for low-paying jobs between marginalized lower socioeconomic groups in part structures the "new forms" that racial discourse in the United States has taken in the last decade of the twentieth century. Concurrently, residual feelings and national and regional histories around racial and ethnic difference still motivate much of contemporary social relations. For film and television to suggest that race has "disappeared" from the enactment of public and private life is a form of impolitic denial.

Contemporary audiences engage films through their own cultural and psychic anxieties about sexual and racial difference, anxieties that are informed by other cultural intersections of race and sexuality. At the same time, scenarios of heterosexual, interracial relations played out on contemporary screens share a number of propensities with classical scenarios.[13] Mainstream films and television continue to deploy "a variety of narrative and visual 'strategies of containment'" that persist in confirming the politics of racial difference.[14]

Despite the changes in production and viewing practices and sites, movie stars continue to occupy a similar place in the public's imagination and in consumer culture as they did sixty years ago, when del Río was featured on the screens of the local movie palace and on the pages of *Photoplay*. Even if spectators are qualitatively and fundamentally different, spectatorship is still linked to individual and cultural processes of desire.

At the same time, the various media apparatuses still function as "safe zones" wherein viewers are free to engage with the text in exploring fears and desires that are politically and discursively repressed in public life.[15] If, as Carol Clover suggests, "gender displacement can provide a kind of identificatory buffer, an emotional remove that permits the majority audience to explore taboo subjects in the relative safety of vicariousness," then might not "racial displacement" provide similar kinds of liberating identificatory mechanisms?[16]

Jackie Stacey suggests that "spectator/star relationships all concern the interplay between self and ideal," and that these relationships "can be seen to articulate homoerotic desires." For Stacey, "recognizing oneself as different from, yet also as similar to, a feminine ideal other" produces pleasure in difference. While Stacey acknowledges the necessary distinction between desire and identification, she argues that the "rigid" theoretical distinction between the two processes "has made it very difficult to conceptualize the complexity of spectator/star relationships."[17]

Taking Stacey's point as ground for a new reading strategy, then, if we substitute race for gender, "blackness" or "brownness" for "femininity," might it be possible to theorize alternative spectatorial relations that could produce transformations in the material world? If, as feminist theorists such as Clover and Berenstein have suggested, spectatorship relies to some extent on cross-gendered identification, then there is a possibility that it also relies on cross-racial identification. While recognizing the real power of hegemonic discourses, I also want to acknowledge the fluidity and fragility of identificatory structures of spectatorship and of identity. While on one hand racial and ethnic movie stars stand in as powerful iconic embodiments of difference, on the other hand they offer spectators the pleasures of difference, pleasures that might, potentially, offer a space for the transformation of social identities and relations.

# Notes

## Introduction

1. *Photoplay,* February 1933, 74. I have used the proper Spanish spelling of del Río's name throughout, except where quoting from U.S. sources that did not use the accent in the original publications.

2. Similarly, in her study of Mae West, Ramona Curry does not examine "the person and performer, but rather the sustained interest in 'Mae West' as a popular American icon" even after her death. Curry is not interested in writing a biography of West, but instead takes "biographies as an instance of 'Mae West'—a popular media phenomenon that has generated a range of functions and meanings in U.S. cultural history." Ramona Curry, *Too Much of a Good Thing: Mae West as Cultural Icon* (Minneapolis: University of Minnesota Press, 1996), xv, xiv.

3. I use the term *racialized sexuality,* following JanMohamed's definition, to indicate "the point where the deployment of sexuality intersects with the deployment of race." See Abdul R. JanMohamed, "Sexuality on/of the Racial Border: Foucault, Wright, and the Articulation of 'Racialized Sexuality,'" in *Discourses of Sexuality: From Aristotle to Aids,* ed. Domna C. Stanton (Ann Arbor: University of Michigan Press, 1992), 94.

4. For example, tracing Western representations of sexuality from the Middle Ages up through the present, Sander L. Gilman finds that race and sexuality are inexorably linked. Gilman locates sexuality in human fantasies about what different

genitalia "looked like, fantasies" that "are in no way separate from the other sys-tems of bodily representation" such as skin color. Sander L. Gilman, *Difference and Pathology: Stereotypes of Sexuality, Race and Madness* (Ithaca, N.Y.: Cornell University Press, 1985), 8–10.

5. Umberto Eco, writing of another kind of performer, a "drunkard exposed in a public place by the Salvation Army," reminds us that "the drunken man has lost his original nature of 'real' body among real bodies. He is no more a world object among world objects—he has become a semiotic device." Umberto Eco, *The Limits of Interpretation* (Bloomington: Indiana University Press, 1990), 102.

6. Conventions of casting and screen performance in Hollywood cinema impose some limits on the meaning of a star in a particular film. Barry King writes that whereas on one hand typecasting "ties the actor as it were to biological and social destiny," on the other hand, meaning is inhibited by the "suppression of those elements of the actor's appearance and behavior that are not intended to mean at the level of the characterization." King points to factors such as "hair colour, body shape, repertoire of gestures, registers of speech, accent, dialect." Barry King, "Articulating Stardom" in *Stardom: Industry of Desire,* ed. Christine Gledhill (London: Routledge, 1991), 173.

Conversely, Andrew Britton is interested in the restrictions that genre conven-tions dictate. He argues that although the star's role in a particular film may be dis-tinct, her star text is tied up with certain concepts she has "at various times embod-ied" in genre films. For Britton, stars such as John Wayne, Gary Cooper, James Stewart, Henry Fonda, and Clint Eastwood "cannot be discussed significantly with-out reference to the concept of the Western hero . . . or to the tensions within the myth of white American history, refracted through a specific contemporary mo-ment, which the genre articulates." Britton insists, therefore, that a star's presence in a film has generic, dramatic, and ideological implications that may or may not inter-sect. Thus, according to Britton, it is fundamentally important to differentiate and situate a star's function in relation to a particular film rather then assume a coher-ent, unchanging star text. Andrew Britton, "Stars and Genre," also in *Stardom,* 202.

Although I agree, in general, with King and Britton's assertions, in the case of racial and ethnic stars their argument falls short. Hair can be dyed, cut, or im-planted; weight can be lost or gained, mannerisms and speech patterns can be learned; gender can be disguised; John Wayne can play a cowboy or a soldier. However, the physical markers that signify cultural conception of racial and ethnic difference are not as easily concealed. Paul Robeson and Dorothy Dandridge's blackness *could never be disarticulated from their star texts* regardless of the charac-ters they embodied in films or the genres within which the films were located.

7. Donald Kirihara. "The Accepted Idea Displaced: Stereotype and Sessue Hayakawa," in *The Birth of Whiteness: Race and the Emergence of U.S. Cinema,* ed. Daniel Bernardi (New Brunswick, N.J.: Rutgers University Press, 1996), 81–82.

8. Etienne Balibar and Immanuel Wallerstein, *Race, Nation and Class: Am-biguous Identities* (London: Verso, 1994).

9. E. Ann Kaplan points out that Hollywood "is not a national cinema, but a universal or global one" and that its films "insist that Hollywood is not about Americans and American life specifically, but about all human life and behavior." However, Hollywood's vision of "human life" is grounded in ideologies of an American national identity as opposed to other geographically, culturally, and racially different identities. For Hollywood, American "human stories" are, ipso facto, "universal human stories" and, therefore, ideologies of race, racial difference, and racialized sexuality are "universal." E. Ann Kaplan, *Looking for the Other: Feminism, Film, and the Imperial Gaze* (New York: Routledge, 1997), 57.

10. Richard Dyer remarks on the obvious: "To represent people is to represent bodies." Richard Dyer, *White* (London: Routledge, 1997), 14. According to Dyer, "Race is always about bodies," whether it is couched in terms of blood, genes, heredity, or bodily characteristics (24).

11. Michel Foucault's writings describe the production and expansion of modern discourses about the body, including sexuality, corporal punishment, and medical and mental pathology over the past three centuries.

12. Linda Williams argues that this cinematic study "quickly became a powerful fantasization of the body of woman." Linda Williams, "Film Body: An Implantation of Perversions," in *Narrative, Apparatus, Ideology,* ed. Philip Rosen (New York: Columbia University Press, 1986), 532. Looking at the work of Eadweard Muybridge and Georges Méliès, Williams writes that "nowhere has the deployment of sexuality and its attendant implantation of perversions been more evident than in the visible intensification of the body that came about with the invention of cinema" (508).

13. Kaplan, *Looking for the Other*, 4.

14. Ibid., 9.

15. Karen Alexander discusses the positioning of Dorothy Dandridge as "Hollywood's first love goddess of colour" and Hollywood's continuing resistance to allow Dandridge to escape this category. Karen Alexander, "Fatal Beauties: Black Women in Hollywood," in *Stardom: Industry of Desire,* ed. Christine Gledhill (London: Routledge, 1991), 52.

16. Paul Robeson's accomplishments and successes in American culture and the American marketplace challenged scientific and popular discourses about race and racial characteristics of blacks in general. Despite the dominance of racist beliefs and practices, Robeson crossed the color line in American popular culture and moved beyond the "accepted" limits of black stardom in the eyes of his audiences. Faced with the dilemma of a black man who attended both Rutgers and Columbia Universities and succeeded as a football champion and a film star, one critic "could only conclude that Negroes seemed to be 'natural born actors.'" Quoted in Michael E. Parrish, *Anxious Decades: America in Prosperity and Depression, 1920–1941* (New York: W. W. Norton, 1992), 135. For a discussion of Robeson's star text, see Richard Dyer, "Paul Robeson: Crossing Over," in *Heavenly Bodies: Film Stars and Society* (New York: St. Martin's, 1986).

17. Richard deCordova writes that an actor's "existence outside of films emerged merely as an extension of an existence already laid out within films," an existence confirmed through a "tautological loop." Richard deCordova, *Picture Personalities: The Emergence of the Star System in America* (Urbana: University of Illinois Press, 1990), 85, 91.

18. Dyer has argued that "the technology of lighting and the specific mode of [Hollywood] movie lighting have racial implications." He asserts, in fact, that Hollywood cinematographers "light for whiteness." *White*, 84, 89.

19. Ana López contends that del Río's "'otherness' was located and defined on a sexual rather than an ethnic register." However, I am arguing here that because del Río's "ethnic register" is undeniably obvious, her meaning for American audiences is much more complex. Ana M. López, "Are All Latins from Manhattan? Hollywood, Ethnography and Cultural Colonialism," in *Unspeakable Images: Ethnicity and the American Cinema*, ed. Lester D. Friedman (Urbana: University of Illinois Press, 1991), 410.

## 1. Inventing Dolores del Río

1. Lynn Dumenil, *The Modern Temper: American Culture and Society in the 1920s* (New York: Hill & Wang, 1995), 119.

2. *Information Service* 32 (April 4, 1953): 2–3, reprinted in *Immigration and the United States*, ed. Poyntz Tyler (New York: H. W. Wilson, 1956), 29.

3. Antonio Ríos-Bustamante, "Latino Participation in the Hollywood Film Industry, 1911–45," in *Chicanos and Film: Representation and Resistance*, ed. Chon A. Noriega (Minneapolis: University of Minnesota Press, 1992), 20. Ríos-Bustamante suggests that full-scale racial exclusion took some time, because many European immigrant directors had not yet internalized the racial attitudes of Anglo-Americans—this was something the Jewish and German directors had to "learn" (20).

4. Daniel Bernardi argues that racial stereotypes in the earliest films of "Selig, Lubin, Paley, Porter, the American Biograph Company, and the Edison Manufacturing Company . . . can be seen as causal factors behind the cinematic categorizing of non-whites as inferior and whites as superior." Daniel Bernardi, "The Voice of Whiteness: D. W. Griffith's Biograph Films (1908–1913)," in *The Birth of Whiteness: Race and the Emergence of U.S. Cinema*, ed. Daniel Bernardi (New Brunswick, N.J.: Rutgers University Press, 1996), 125.

5. Michael Rogin, "Making America Home: Racial Masquerade and Ethnic Assimilation in the Transition to Talking Pictures," *Journal of American History* 79 (December 1992): 1052.

6. Ibid., 1052–53.

7. Ríos-Bustamante, "Latino Participation," 7.

8. Gaylyn Studlar, *This Mad Masquerade: Stardom and Masculinity in the Jazz Age* (New York: Columbia University Press, 1996), 178.

9. Ríos-Bustamante, "Latino Participation," 20.

10. Ibid., 19–21. Ríos-Bustamante argues that although these roles did allow some to become stars, this opportunity had positive and negative consequences. He notes, for example, that on the one hand these roles as "stars" emphasized the beauty of Latino/a peoples; on the other hand, they reinforced existing racial prejudices and stereotypes.

11. Ivan St. Johns, "A Daughter of the Dons," *Photoplay,* June 1927, 67; photo caption, *Photoplay,* August 1927, 44; "Two Girls Who Succeeded," *Photoplay,* September 1927, 48.

12. Contrast del Río's career with that of the Brazilian actress Carmen Miranda, who, according to Ana M. López, "travels and is inserted into different landscapes, but she remains the same from film to film, purely Latin American." Ana M. López, "Are All Latins from Manhattan? Hollywood, Ethnography and Cultural Colonialism," in *Unspeakable Images: Ethnicity and the American Cinema,* ed. Lester D. Friedman (Urbana: University of Illinois Press, 1991), 410.

13. Tom Gunning, *D. W. Griffith and the Origins of American Narrative Film: The Early Years at Biograph* (Urbana: University of Illinois Press, 1994), 11.

14. Giuliana Bruno, *Streetwalking on a Ruined Map: Cultural Theory and the City Films of Elvira Notari* (Princeton, N.J.: Princeton University Press, 1993), 3–4.

15. Studlar, *This Mad Masquerade,* 5.

16. Michel de Certeau, *The Writing of History* (New York: Columbia University Press, 1988). Historiography is a "site of production" that is circumscribed by three crucial relations: the social, cultural, and historical place of the historian; a modus operandi of historical inquiry and interpretation; and conventions of academic writing. According to de Certeau, historiography, the writing of history, "has ceased to be the representation of a providential time, that is of a history decided by an inaccessible Subject. . . . [It now] takes the position of the subject of action . . . whose objective is to 'make history'" (57).

17. Janet Staiger, *Interpreting Films: Studies in the Historical Reception of American Cinema* (Princeton, N.J.: Princeton University Press, 1992), 80.

18. Ibid., 81.

19. Dumenil, *The Modern Temper,* 6–13.

20. Ibid., 99.

21. Kathy Peiss, *Hope in a Jar: The Making of America's Beauty Culture* (New York: Henry Holt, 1998), 135.

22. Dumenil, *The Modern Temper,* 57, 58.

23. Ibid., 95.

24. For example, see "Shopping Service," *Photoplay,* May 1925, 49–53.

25. Peiss cites a study of the influence of movies conducted by sociologist Herbert Blumer in the 1920s and 1930s. According to the study, "three-fourths of the 'delinquent girls' said they heightened their sex appeal by imitating movie stars' clothes, hair, and cosmetics." According to Peiss, women's relationship to movie stars "was less direct imitation than a negotiation between one's sense of self and the ideal female images." *Hope in a Jar,* 191.

26. Ibid., 97.

27. Ibid., 152. Michael E. Parrish writes that "the number [of women] who patronized beauty parlors for manicures, permanent waves, and hair-dying grew at an astonishing pace. . . . By 1930 the cosmetics industry had grown from $17 million a year to over $200 million." Michael E. Parrish, *Anxious Decades: America in Prosperity and Depression, 1920–1941* (New York: W. W. Norton, 1992), 151–52.

28. One article advised, for example, that "long sleeves, lace collars and cuffs, and a jabot" will absorb dishwater and that "tennis can be torture in long sleeves, a wool skirt that is tight over the hips and rubber soled sandals." Instead, the writer recommended "a pretty apron, comfortable shoes and a pair of rubber gloves" for the kitchen and "a white sleeveless frock, with a full pleated skirt and regulation tennis shoes" for the courts. "How to Dress for Trying Roles," *Photoplay*, March 1928, 66–67.

29. Peiss, *Hope in a Jar*, 136.

30. For singular analyses of the male "exotic" star of the 1920s, see Studlar, *This Mad Masquerade*; Miriam Hansen, *Babel and Babylon: Spectatorship in American Silent Film* (Cambridge: Harvard University Press, 1991).

31. According to Peiss, the cosmetic industry employed a strategy of pitching different products to different "beauty types." This strategy "offered a means of perceiving and classifying the dizzying array of complexions in a nation of immigrants." Peiss discusses a promotional campaign by Max Factor that employed Lupe Vélez and Ramón Novarro to promote "society make-up" to Latinas in *La Opinión*, a Los Angeles-based Spanish-language newspaper. *Hope in a Jar*, 148–49.

32. Fatimah Tobing Rony, *The Third Eye: Race, Cinema, and Ethnographic Spectacle* (Durham, N.C.: Duke University Press, 1996), 6.

33. Peiss, *Hope in a Jar*, 148.

34. For an explanation of the workings of studio publicity departments in the 1920s and 1930s, see Thomas Harris, "The Building of Popular Images: Grace Kelly and Marilyn Monroe," in *Stardom: Industry of Desire*, ed. Christine Gledhill (London: Routledge, 1991).

35. David Ramón, *Historia de un rostro* (Mexico City: CCH Dirección Plantel Sur, 1993), 54.

36. Margery Wilson, *Dolores Del Rio* (Los Angeles: Chines, 1928), 10–11.

37. Her husband, Jaime del Río, unable to further his own career as a screenwriter, moved to Europe and the marriage fell apart. His wife initiated divorce proceedings at the same time that Carewe was divorcing his wife, and rumors were flying.

38. Dolores del Río to Edwin Carewe, January 19, 1927; del Río to W. R. Sheehan, January 19, 1927; both from 20th Century Fox Collection 095, Records of the Legal Department, Box FX-LR-021, "Dolores del Río," Arts and Special Collections Library, University of California, Los Angeles.

39. "*Loves of Carmen* with Dolores del Río and Victor McLaglen," *Photoplay*, November 1927, 9.

40. "Dolores del Río in the Title Role of Carmen," *Photoplay,* November 1927, 9.

41. "Walsh Starts Filming on Fox Film, 'Carmen,'" *Exhibitors Herald,* January 29, 1927.

42. Among the prohibitions were pointed profanity; licentious or suggestive nudity; portrayal of illegal traffic in drugs; portrayal of sex hygiene and venereal diseases; scenes of actual childbirth; scenes showing children's sex organs; ridicule of the clergy or willful offense to any nation, race, or creed; and a portrayal of sexual perversion, white slavery, or miscegenation (the sexual mixing of races). Leff and Simmons note in their study of the Production Code that many producers rejected what they deemed outside interference and "scribbled RETURN TO SENDER across the envelope." Leonard J. Leff and Jerold L. Simmons, *The Dame in the Kimono: Hollywood, Censorship, and the Production Code from the 1920s to the 1960s* (New York: Grove Weidenfeld, 1990), 7.

43. Edwin Carewe to Sol Wurtzel, November 7, 1927, 20th Century Fox Collection.

44. Jason S. Joy to Carl E. Milliken, n.d.; Gunther R. Lessing to Edwin Carewe, n.d.; both in 20th Century Fox Collection.

45. *Photoplay,* June 1927, 66.

46. *Photoplay,* July 1927, 69.

47. Gary D. Keller, *Hispanics and United States Film: An Overview and Handbook* (Tempe, Ariz.: Bilingual Press, 1994), 40. As Keller notes, male roles were more varied: the greaser, the bandit, the Bad Mexican, the Gay Caballero, the Good or Faithful Mexican, the Good Badman, and the Hispanic Avenger (40–67).

48. Abel, review of *Pals First, Variety* August 25, 1926.

49. Chon A. Noriega, "Birth of the Southwest: Social Protest, Tourism, and D. W. Griffith's *Ramona,*" in *The Birth of Whiteness: Race and the Emergence of U.S. Cinema,* ed. Daniel Bernardi (New Brunswick, N.J.: Rutgers University Press, 1996), 217.

50. The first film adaptation of Ramona was directed by D.W. Griffith in 1910; a second, directed by Lloyd Brown, came out in 1916; and a subsequent remake, directed by Henry King and starring Loretta Young, was released by 20th Century Fox in 1936. Ibid., 203–26.

51. Ibid., 210–11.

52. Noriega writes that "films from [Griffith's] *Ramona* to *Duel in the Sun* . . . can be said to 'deconstruct' the historical Mexican and Mexican-American subject, bifurcating a mestizo or mixed-race identity into its constituent parts." Ibid., 217.

53. In the novel, Ramona is the half-breed daughter of a Scotsman who had been in love with Señora Moreno's elder sister.

54. See review of *Ramona, Exhibitors Herald,* March 2, 1927; Land, review of *Ramona, Variety,* May 16, 1928. *Photoplay*'s reviewer laments "the entire elimination of Ramona's life from the time she runs away with Allessandro, her Indian lover, until her child dies." Review of *Ramona, Photoplay,* March 1928, 52.

55. "The Shadow Stage: A Review of New Pictures," *Photoplay,* March 1928, 52.

56. Ibid.

57. *Exhibitors Herald,* March 2, 1927.

58. For a discussion of the ways in which the MPPDA mediated the relations between Hollywood and foreign markets, see Ruth Vasey, *The World According to Hollywood, 1918–1939* (Madison: University of Wisconsin Press, 1997).

59. Ibid., 38.

60. Major F. L. Herron to Jason S. Joy, April 18, 1927, 20th Century Fox Collection. Joy responded immediately: "I have taken the subject of 'Ramona' up with Edwin Carewe and his scenarist who tell me it will be guided by our advice. They are grateful for the time, without which they probably would have made careless mistakes which might have been costly. Keep shooting them to me—I am a good errand boy and I like it." Joy to Herron, April 28, 1927, 20th Century Fox Collection.

61. Helen Delpar, "Goodbye to the Greaser: Mexico, the MPPDA, and Derogatory Films, 1922–1926," *Journal of Popular Film and Television* 12, no. 1 (1984): 36. Given *Ramona's* theme, it is also important to note that by the 1920s, Mexican immigrants made up a significant segment of Hollywood's audience in places like Texas, New Mexico, and Southern California. To be sure, that audience was diverse. Many of these people claimed familial roots back to Spanish land grants, whereas others were newly arrived agricultural workers.

62. Vasey argues that the Mexican problem "helped in several ways to bring home to the American producers the implications of their participation in global distribution." *The World According to Hollywood,* 19.

63. Delpar, "Goodbye to the Greaser," 39–40.

64. Rogin criticizes Werner Sollers's conflation of race and ethnicity, writing that American citizenship "created a mystic national body that insisted on distinctions of blood." Rogin acknowledges that "ethnic groups shared with peoples of color both racially based nativist hostility and the loss of home." But he argues that, eventually, "ethnic minorities were propelled into the melting pot by the progress that kept racial minorities out." Michael P. Rogin, *Black Face, White Noise: Jewish Immigrants in the Hollywood Melting Pot* (Berkeley: University of California Press, 1996), 55.

## 2. Race and Romance

1. Alexander Walker, *Stardom: The Hollywood Phenomenon* (New York: Stein & Day, 1970), 211.

2. Although Walker notes that "it was suspected that a professional singer" stood in for del Río, the point is that audiences believed it was really the actress singing. Ibid., 212.

3. Ibid., 227. Aside from the increased costs of producing individual sound pictures, the studios were forced to refit their production systems, and movie theaters had to be converted for sound.

4. Richard Maltby and Ian Craven, *Hollywood Cinema* (Oxford: Blackwell, 1995), 160.

5. Ibid., 163.

6. "The Charmer Who Enslaved a King," *Photoplay*, August 1934, 43.

7. Richard Watts Jr., "On the Screen," *New York Herald Tribune*, September 12, 1932, 8; quoted in Michael E. Parrish, *Anxious Decades: America in Prosperity and Depression, 1920–1941* (New York: W. W. Norton, 1992), 26. Other reviews often mistook the film's actual location. The reviewer for *Time*, August 22, 1932, called the film a "pleasant little lesson in Hawaiian without tears" located "at Tahiti" (20). The *Motion Picture Herald*, June 25, 1932, located the film in Polynesia (25), and *Film Daily*, August 6, 1932, described Luana as a "Hawaiian" princess (3). A number of reviews pointed to the strangeness of the island's inhabitants. A reviewer for the *New Yorker*, September 13, 1932, for example, found the native ceremonials very "oo-la-la in the wild abandon of the hula girls and the not less eloquent wriggles of the men Kanakas" (53).

8. The "whitening" of the nonwhite love object was a narrative practice formulated in colonial transracial love stories. Mary Louise Pratt notes that in those narratives "the conventional facial sketch of the non-European love object distinguishes her or him from the stereotypic portraits of slaves and savages." In the eighteenth century, this strategy worked as both a justification of the erotic appeal of a nonwhite, colonized subject and a neutralization of the violence of colonialist practices such as slavery. Mary Louise Pratt, *Imperial Eyes: Travel Writing and Transculturation* (London: Routledge, 1992), 100–101. As Pratt puts it, "Romantic love was a good a device as any for 'embracing'" colonized peoples for political purposes (101). For a discussion of the emergence of colonial fictional and nonfictional modes of "transracial love stories" in the late eighteenth century, see *Imperial Eyes*, chap. 5.

9. See Richard Dyer, *White* (London: Routledge, 1997), for a discussion of the "racial character of [cinematic] technologies." Dyer explains how the technologies of photography and Hollywood cinema have historically lent themselves to "privileging white people" by developing techniques and conventions that favored "lighting for whiteness" (83–84).

10. Michael Omi and Howard Winant, *Racial Formation in the United States: From the 1960s to the 1990s*, 2d ed. (New York: Routledge, 1994), 14–15.

11. Mary Ann Doane, "Dark Continents: Epistemologies of Racial and Sexual Difference in Psychoanalysis and the Cinema," in *Femmes Fatales: Feminism, Film Theory, Psychoanalysis* (London: Routledge, 1991), 215.

12. E. Ann Kaplan, *Looking for the Other: Feminism, Film, and the Imperial Gaze* (New York: Routledge, 1997), 73.

13. My discussion in this section is very much influenced by Ann Laura Stoler's *Race and the Education of Desire: Foucault's History of Sexuality and the Colonial Order of Things* (Durham, N.C.: Duke University Press, 1995).

14. Virginia Maxwell, "The 'New Deal' in Girls," *Photoplay*, September 1933, 34.

15. Ibid. Peiss has noted that the second generation of immigrant women, daughters born in the United States, "put on make-up to look 'American,' expressing

their new sense of national identity and personal freedom." Kathy Peiss, *Hope in a Jar: The Making of America's Beauty Culture* (New York: Henry Holt, 1998), 188.

16. Cal Yorks, "The Monthly Broadcast from Hollywood," *Photoplay,* January 1933, 124.

17. Evaline Lieber, "What Price Stardom?" *Photoplay,* September, 1932, 57.

18. Quoted in Ruth Rankin, "13 Irresistible Women," *Photoplay,* August 1934, 98.

19. See Charles Eckert, "The Carole Lombard in Macy's Window," and Charlotte Cornelia Herzog and Jane Marie Gaines, " 'Puffed Sleeves before Teatime': Joan Crawford, Adrian and Women Audiences," both in *Stardom: Industry of Desire,* ed. Christine Gledhill (London: Routledge, 1991), for discussion of the relationship between Hollywood and fashion industries in the 1930s. Both essays note that Hollywood used fashion to attract female audiences while fashion industries used Hollywood to advertise "ready-made" versions of the clothing stars wore in their films.

20. Carolyn Van Wyck, "Hollywood's Beauty Shop," *Photoplay,* October 1933, 77.

21. Carolyn Van Wyck, "First Aid for the Gift Shopping List," *Photoplay,* January 1934, 94; Sylvia of Hollywood, "You, Too, Can Have the Beauty Secret I Gave Dolores del Río," *Photoplay,* January 1934, 101.

22. Photo caption, *Photoplay,* February 1933, 74.

23. Gina Marchetti discusses a number of early films about interracial affairs. She proposes that films such as *The Wrath of the Gods* (1914), *The Cheat* (1915), *Madame Butterfly* (1915), *Broken Blossoms* (1919), and *The Forbidden City* (1918) "simultaneously warn against miscegenation while celebrating romantic love." Gina Marchetti, "Tragic and Transcendent Love in *The Forbidden City,*" in *The Birth of Whiteness: Race and the Emergence of U.S. Cinema,* ed. Daniel Bernardi (New Brunswick, N.J.: Rutgers University Press, 1996), 257.

24. Vidor's film was released two years before Hays's list of "Don'ts and Be Carefuls" was "officially" adopted as the Motion Picture Production Code. See chapter 4 for a discussion of the effects of the Code on film content.

25. Advertisement for *Bird of Paradise, Motion Picture Herald,* September 17, 1932, 23.

26. Ibid.

27. This "official" stance was later clarified. Shohat and Stam cite a 1937 *Handbook for Motion Picture Writers and Reviewers* that states, "The union of a member of the Polynesians and allied races of the Island groups with a member of the white race is not ordinarily considered a miscegenetic relationship." Ella Shohat and Robert Stam, *Unthinking Eurocentrism: Multiculturalism and the Media* (London: Routledge, 1994), 143.

28. Although after 1934 observance of the Production Code was optional, not legally enforceable, and thus often ignored, miscegenation was a line that was rarely crossed in Hollywood cinema. When it was, the "abnormal" relation was

abandoned in favor of monogamous heterosexuality within strictly defined racial categories. In *Looking for the Other,* Kaplan suggests that films that featured "the attraction of exotic women of color for white males" displaced the historical attraction of white masters for their African American female slaves (74). I argue that this notion of displacement may be limiting, given the racial divisions between whites and all other nonwhite people.

29. See David R. Roediger, *The Wages of Whiteness: Race and the Making of the American Working Class* (New York: Verso, 1991), 155–56. Up until the 1860s, the term *amalgamation* had been used to describe racial mixing. According to Roediger, miscegenation became part of American popular discourse in 1863 as a "pivotal issue in the 1864 presidential campaign" (155). Democrats D. G. Croly and George Wakeman anonymously published a seemingly abolitionist pamphlet, designed to impugn and discredit Republican abolitionist candidates, titled *Miscegenation: The Theory of the Blending of the Races, Applied to the American White Man and Negro.*

30. Ramona Curry, *Too Much of a Good Thing: Mae West as Cultural Icon* (Minneapolis: University of Minnesota Press, 1996), 15, 16. Michael Rogin points to a number of Hollywood films of the 1920s that sympathetically portray ethnic intermarriage. He asserts that films like *Old San Francisco* (a 1927 film that depicts the marriage between a girl of "old Spanish" ancestry and an Irish American) "repudiated nativist prejudice." However, the villain in this movie is still a "racial" villain, an "Oriental passing as white." For Rogin, this narrative resolution "illustrates the process Michel Foucault has described that substitutes one exclusion for another." In the case of *Old San Francisco,* miscegenation is facilitated between "whites divided by ethnic lines" rather than race. Michael P. Rogin, "Making America Home: Racial Masquerade and Ethnic Assimilation in the Transition to Talking Pictures," *Journal of American History* 79 (December 1992): 1059.

31. The *Motion Picture Herald,* January 28, 1933, comments on one scene it finds "distasteful," describing the scene as one in which "Del Rio sucks an orange and transfers the juice from her mouth into McCrea's to quench his thirst while he is unconscious" (50). *Collier's* magazine wrote that the "Don'ts and Be Carefuls" really meant "'Don't forget to stop before you have gone to far' and 'If you can't be good, be careful.'" Quoted in Ruth A. Inglis, *Freedom of the Movies: A Report on Self-Regulation from the Commission on Freedom of the Press* (Chicago: University of Chicago Press, 1947), 116.

32. *Tabu: A Story of the South Seas,* another "South Seas" film released a year earlier, directed by the German émigré F. W. Murnau, also features a native princess who is sexually "tabu." The narratives of the two films follow a similar trajectory: the romance of two innocent young people. Although, as in *Bird of Paradise,* the "central confrontation" in *Tabu* is that of "desire versus law," the question of miscegenation does not figure at all in Murnau's film. See Fatimah Tobing Rony, *The Third Eye: Race, Cinema, and Ethnographic Spectacle* (Durham, N.C.: Duke University Press, 1996), 151. However, *Tabu's* fundamental "moral message,"

that "the indigenous person who does not remain in his or her proper space is something abhorrent" (155), also describes the major theme of *Bird of Paradise*.

33. Shohat and Stam, *Unthinking Eurocentrism*, 143.

34. Charles Musser notes that, for newly arrived immigrants, the new American urban space was their first encounter with ethnic diversity, an encounter that "threw up a complex of psychological feelings toward others." Charles Musser, "Ethnicity, Role-Playing, and American Film Comedy: From *Chinese Laundry Scene* to *Whoopee* (1894–1930)," in *Unspeakable Images: Ethnicity and the American Cinema*, ed. Lester D. Friedman (Urbana: University of Illinois Press, 1991), 42.

35. Rony points out, for example, that *King Kong* (1933) is more than just a "cinematic fantasy . . . [but] in significant respects builds on and redeploys themes borrowed from the scientific time machine of anthropology." *The Third Eye*, 159.

36. Homi K. Bhabha, "The Other Question: Homi K. Bhabha Reconsiders the Stereotype and Colonial Discourse," *Screen* 24, no. 6 (1983): 30.

37. See Doane, "Dark Continents," 214.

38. Shohat and Stam, among others, discuss the way in which these cinematic representations of the West's exploration of non-Western lands are gender coded within structural relations of power: the other is eroticized, exoticized, and feminized, whereas the Western (male) explorer is described as the "cultivator" and "fertilizer" (of barren lands) and the "penetrator" (of virgin territory). *Unthinking Eurocentrism*, 141–45.

39. Kaplan, *Looking for the Other*, 69–70.

40. Ibid., 80.

41. According to Pratt, "the lesson to be learned from colonial love stories" is that even though the lovers challenge colonial and racial hierarchies, "in the end they acquiesce to them." *Imperial Eyes*, 97. As will be seen, this is the fate of Johnny and Luana in *Bird of Paradise*.

42. Lynn Dumenil, *The Modern Temper: American Culture and Society in the 1920s* (New York: Hill & Wang, 1995), 130.

43. The majority of female workers came from the working class and found jobs in the lower-paid, lower-status sectors of the economy—primarily clerical, retail, manufacturing, and domestic work (ibid., 112–14). Duminel notes further that "the types of jobs available to young women varied according to race and ethnicity" (ibid., 113).

44. Ibid., 112.

45. Rhona J. Berenstein, *Attack of the Leading Ladies: Gender, Sexuality, and Spectatorship in Classic Horror Cinema* (New York: Columbia University Press, 1996), 15, 16.

46. Marchetti, "Tragic and Transcendent Love."

47. Stoler writes that "the myth of blood may be traced, as Foucault does, from an aristocratic preoccupation with legitimacy, pure blood, and descent. . . . It was equally dependent on an imperial politics of exclusion that was worked out earlier and reworked later on colonial ground." *Race and the Education of Desire*, 51.

48. Letter to the editor, *Photoplay*, April 1932, 15.

49. "Showmen's Reviews," *Motion Picture Herald*, June 25, 1932, 25. The *Motion Picture Herald* describes its "Showmen's Reviews" section as the "department that deals with new product from the point of view of the exhibitor who is to purvey it to his own public." Exhibitors are advised that *Bird of Paradise* provides them with "plenty to sell—heart-touching drama, brilliant romance, a Dolores del Río, passionate yet retaining the simplicity and sweetness of a girl to whom the kiss of civilization was an exotic thrill."

50. See Michel Foucault, *History of Sexuality*, vol. 1, *An Introduction* (New York: Vintage, 1990), 36–49.

51. Ibid., 36–37.

52. Abdul JanMohamed writes that "racialized sexuality, unlike its bourgeois counterpart, links power and knowledge in a negative, inverse relation: the perpetuation of white patriarchy and the preservation of its self-image require that it deny a 'scientific-discursive' knowledge of its sexual violation of the racial border." Abdul R. JanMohamed, "Sexuality on/of the Racial Border: Foucault, Wright, and the Articulation of 'Racialized Sexuality,'" in *Discourses of Sexuality: From Aristotle to AIDS*, ed. Domna C. Stanton (Ann Arbor: University of Michigan Press, 1992), 102.

53. Lea Jacobs, *The Wages of Sin: Censorship and the Fallen Woman Film, 1928–1942* (Madison: University of Wisconsin Press, 1991), 21, 23.

54. Ibid., chap. 2.

## 3. Uncomfortably Real

I am indebted to Daniel Bernardi for suggesting the title for this chapter, which is revised from an essay published in his edited anthology *Classic Whiteness: Race and the Hollywood Studio System* (Minneapolis: University of Minnesota Press, forthcoming).

1. Ruth Vasey, *The World According to Hollywood, 1918–1939* (Madison: University of Wisconsin Press, 1997), 101.

2. Vasey notes, for example, that "by 1934 consultations [between Mexican officials and representatives of the Production Code Administration] took place as a matter of course." Ruth Vasey, "Foreign Parts: Hollywood's Global Distribution and the Representation of Ethnicity," in *Movie Censorship and American Culture*, ed. Francis G. Couvares (Washington, D.C.: Smithsonian Institution Press, 1996), 227.

3. For an analysis of how international markets and politics shaped Hollywood's national, racial, and ethnic representations, see Vasey, *The World According to Hollywood*.

4. Vasey notes that "between the world wars the industry consistently derived about 35 percent of its gross revenue from export earnings." "Foreign Parts," 213.

5. Gerald D. Nash, *The Great Depression and World War II: Organizing America, 1933–1945* (New York: St. Martin's, 1979), 19.

6. Jack Alicoate, "Introduction," in *Film Daily Yearbook*, ed. Jack Alicoate (New York: Jack Alicoate, 1930), 3.

7. Jack Alicoate, "Introduction," in *Film Daily Yearbook*, ed. Jack Alicoate (New York: Jack Alicoate, 1933), 3.

8. Andrew W. Bergman, *We're in the Money: Depression America and Its Films* (New York: New York University Press, 1971), xxii.

9. As a cost-cutting measure many actors with less than "star status" were released from their contracts; others saw their salaries slashed. In addition, the studios were personally confronted with a national campaign that rallied around the cry of "America for Americans" when the House Committee on Labor investigated "the high proportion of foreign talent in Hollywood." Alexander Walker, *Stardom: The Hollywood Phenomenon* (New York: Stein & Day, 1970), 242.

10. Robert Sklar, *Movie-Made America: A Cultural History of American Movies* (New York: Random House, 1975), 174.

11. Thomas Schatz, *Hollywood Genres: Formulas, Filmmaking, and the Studio System* (New York: Random House, 1981), 188–89.

12. Sklar, *Movie-Made America*, 175. Charles Eckert notes that the 1933 Warner Bros. musical *42nd Street* "was a boost for the New Deal philosophy of pulling together to whip the depression." According to Eckert, a special train, the "Warner-G.E. Better Times Special," traversed the United States selling optimism, G.E. appliances, and *42nd Street*. Charles Eckert, "The Carole Lombard in Macy's Window," *Quarterly Review of Film Studies* 3, no. 1 (1978): 3.

13. Giuliana Muscio, *Hollywood's New Deal* (Philadelphia: Temple University Press, 1996), 72.

14. As Schatz describes it in *Hollywood Genres*, the musical is focused "around American courtship rites, and the very concept of entertainment" (189). Schatz defines two major categories of the musical: the "backstage" musical, whose plot focuses on the mounting of an elaborate musical show, and the "integrated" musical, "in which lyrics and dance are directly related to the conflicts of the story" (89).

15. Richard Dyer, "Entertainment and Utopia," in *Movies and Methods*, vol. 2, ed. Bill Nichols (Berkeley: University of California Press, 1985), 226, 229.

16. Ella Shohat and Robert Stam, *Unthinking Eurocentrism: Multiculturalism and the Media* (London: Routledge, 1994), 223.

17. Ibid., 126. By this time, Paramount, MGM, 20th Century Fox, Warner Bros., and RKO had established distribution branches in the larger urban centers of Latin America. See Suzanne Mary Donahue, *American Film Distribution: The Changing Marketplace* (Ann Arbor: UMI Research Press, 1987), 143–53.

18. Jorge Schnitman, *Film Industries in Latin America: Dependency and Development* (Norwood, N.J.: Ablex, 1984), 16–17.

19. In the 1930s, the value of U.S. direct investments in Latin America "was much more than twice the value of its investments in any other geographical area of the world." U.S. Department of Commerce, *American Direct Investments in Foreign Countries* (Washington, D.C.: U.S. Government Printing Office, 1930), 18;

quoted in Donald M. Dozer, *Are We Good Neighbors? Three Decades of American Relations, 1930–1960* (Gainesville: University of Florida Press, 1959), 9.

20. B. A. Morgan to Arthur Kelly, April 16, 1930; quoted in Gaizka S. de Usabel, *The High Noon of American Films in Latin America* (Ann Arbor: UMI Research Press, 1982), 103.

21. Vasey, "Foreign Parts," 227–28.

22. Shohat and Stam, *Unthinking Eurocentrism*, 138–39.

23. Katherine Franklin, "Dolores Extols Passive Love," *Photoplay,* April 1934, 39.

24. Gary D. Keller, *Hispanics and United States Film: An Overview and Handbook* (Tempe, Ariz.: Bilingual Press, 1994), 104.

25. Quoted in Franklin, "Dolores Extols Passive Love," 39.

26. *Photoplay,* January 1936, 18.

27. RKO's promotional material for *Flying Down to Rio* focused on the foreign elements of the film: del Río, the carioca, and the tango. *Photoplay* notes that "in the patio scene where she [del Río] sat with a number of American society girls and flirted so dexterously with Gene Raymond . . . the American girls were very frank in their gestures of admiration . . . but del Rio was fascinating. She coquetted with lowered eyes, then she peeped at him through the lattice of her fingers." Franklin, "Dolores Extols Passive Love," 107.

28. Allen L. Woll, *The Latin Image in American Film* (Los Angeles: UCLA Latin American Center Publications, 1980), xxvii.

29. For a discussion of this incident, see Helen Delpar, "Goodbye to the Greaser: Mexico, the MPPDA, and Derogatory Films, 1922–1926," *Journal of Popular Film and Television* 12, no. 1 (1984).

30. Woll, *The Latin Image,* xxix.

31. Ibid.

32. American companies wooed Latin American exhibitors by producing a Spanish-language version of the industry's trade magazine *Motion Picture World.* The new version was called *Cine-Mundial.* In order to deal with the "language problem," Spanish subtitles were screened alongside English-language prints via separate projectors. Ibid., 15.

33. Margarita de Orellana, "The Circular Look: The Incursion of North American Fictional Cinema 1911–1917 into the Mexican Cinema," in *Mediating Two Worlds: Cinematic Encounters in the Americas,* ed. John King, Ana M. López, and Manuel Alvarado (London: British Film Institute, 1993), 10.

34. Ibid., 13.

35. Carlos Monsiváis, "Dolores del Río: The Face as an Institution," in *Mexican Postcards,* trans. John Kraniauskus (London: Verso, 1997), 77.

36. RKO's musicals of the 1930s that featured the team of Fred and Ginger included *Top Hat* (1935), *Follow the Fleet* (1936), *Swing Time* (1936), and *Shall We Dance?* (1937). In *Swing Time,* Rogers also rejects her Latin American boyfriend (portrayed by Georges Metaxa) in favor of her white American suitor, Astaire. Schatz, *Hollywood Genres,* 191.

37. Ibid., 188.

38. Sid, review of *Flying Down to Rio, Variety,* December 26, 1933, 10.

39. Brian Henderson, "A Musical Comedy of Empire," *Film Quarterly* 35, no. 2 (1981–82): 12.

40. Ibid., 4.

41. Sérgio Augusto, "Hollywood Looks at Brazil: From Carmen Miranda to *Moonraker,*" in *Brazilian Cinema,* expanded ed., ed. Randal Johnson and Robert Stam (Berkeley: University of California Press, 1996), 356. See also Henderson, "A Musical Comedy."

42. Dr. James Wingate to Merian C. Cooper, August 26, 1933, in MPAA file, Margaret Herrick Library of the Academy of Motion Picture Arts and Sciences, Beverly Hills, Calif.

43. Production Code Administration to Sidney Kramer, RKO Distributing Corporation, PCA file, Margaret Herrick Library.

44. Ibid.

45. Michael E. Parrish, *Anxious Decades: America in Prosperity and Depression, 1920–1941* (New York: W. W. Norton, 1992), 30.

46. Michael P. Rogin, "Making America Home: Racial Masquerade and Ethnic Assimilation in the Transition to Talking Pictures," *Journal of American History* 79 (December 1992): 1051–53. Rogin offers the example of Al Jolson in blackface in Warner Bros.'s *The Jazz Singer,* writing that "racial cross-dressing supplies 'the Mammy singer' not only with a gentile wife but also with an American past, as plantation nurture replaces the east European home and mother left behind" (1056).

47. Ibid., 1057.

48. Michael P. Rogin, *Black Face, White Noise: Jewish Immigrants in the Hollywood Melting Pot* (Berkeley: University of California Press, 1996), 189.

49. *Madame DuBarry* was the subject of a strident and lengthy battle between Warner Bros. and Joseph I. Breen, director of the PCA. According to Gregory D. Black, Breen felt that the script was so "filled with vulgarity, obscenity and blatant adultery" that it would instigate bad relations with France. Gregory D. Black, *Hollywood Censored: Morality Codes, Catholics, and the Movies* (New York: Cambridge University Press, 1994), 176.

50. *Motion Picture Herald,* June 1, 1935, 43; *Motion Picture Herald,* May 4, 1935, 25–26.

51. "'Caliente Night' Ball or Party, Lets Debs Go Hotcha for Charity," *Motion Picture Herald,* June 1, 1935.

52. Radio script as published in ibid.

53. Review of *In Caliente, Variety,* July 3, 1935, 14. The reviewer also commented that "as a story it's one of those things. As a plug for the Agua Caliente development, Wirt Bowman, Joe Schenck, et al. should underwrite the production cost. It's almost a commercial plug for the Mexican resort across the border from San Diego." Monsiváis, however, calls the film "an oblique denunciation of the

rapacity and shamelessness of Mexicans, eternal strummers of guitars." "Dolores del Río," 77.

54. "Night-Day Beauty Hints Featured," *Photoplay* September 1935; "Hostess in the Modern Manner," *Photoplay,* February 1936, 74.

55. Review of *Devil's Playground, Hollywood Reporter,* February 11, 1937, 3.

56. *Hollywood Reporter,* October 7, 1935, 3.

57. De Usabel, *The High Noon,* 136.

## 4. "Nuestra Dolores"

The title of this chapter comes from the cover of the April 30, 1936, issue of the Spanish-language weekly *Todo,* which featured a close-up of del Río wearing a Mexican hat. The caption under the photo read, "Nuestra Dolores" (Our Dolores).

1. In 1930 she was approached to star in *Santa* but turned it down, and in 1934 the producer Archibald Burns wanted her for *La noche de los mayas,* which was to be directed by del Río's cousin Julio Bracho.

2. Class and racial associations further inflected the term with negative connotations that were made visible in Mexican popular culture such as *fotonovelas* and films from the 1920s forward. In these venues, *pochos* were depicted as illiterate and unskilled lower-class individuals of Indian heritage who lacked social graces and competence. For a discussion of *el pocho,* see Carlos Monsiváis, "De México y los chicanos, de México y su cultura fronteriza," in *La otra cara de México: El pueblo chicano,* ed. David R. Maciel (Mexico City: Ediciones "El Caballito," 1977). According to David R. Maciel, Mexican cinema produced more than one hundred films about the Chicano community, and these Chicano characters were, "with very few exceptions, portrayed as stereotypical *pochos.*" David R. Maciel, "*Pochos* and Other Extremes in Mexican Cinema; or, El Cine Mexicano se va de Bracero, 1922–1963," in *Chicanos and Film: Representation and Resistance,* ed. Chon A. Noriega (Minneapolis: University of Minnesota Press, 1992), 103.

3. "Levantan el boicot a la película 'Viva Villa,'" *Universal,* September 5, 1934. The boycott editorial was submitted by Mexican cinema's main union, the Sindicato de Empleados Cinematografistas del Distrito Federal. On the other hand, in the same issue of *Universal,* Mexican distributors and exhibitors who were dependent on Hollywood films advertised the film as "the spectacle of the day," with major Hollywood stars and "20,000 extras."

4. Gabriel Navarro, "For Mexican Reasons," *Todo,* November 17, 1933.

5. "Regreso tan mexicana como cuando salí de México." Quoted in *Universal,* September 20, 1934. All translations are my own.

6. For an account of del Río's public and private life in Mexico, see David Ramón, *Dolores del Río,* vols. 2 and 3 (Mexico City: Clío, 1997).

7. Emilio García Riera, *El cine Mexicano* (Mexico City: ERA, 1963), 25. The creation of the Banco Cinematográfica (BNC) in 1942 energized the industry. The BNC combined some of the more prominent production and distribution

companies into a single large, integrated firm. This state-controlled bank made loans only to selected private producers associated with the largest studios.

8. Carlos Monsiváis, "Mythologies," in *Mexican Cinema,* ed. Paulo Antonio Paranaguá, trans. Ana M. López (London: British Film Institute, 1995), 117–18.

9. Mexican artists and entrepreneurs had developed smaller studios after the war. In 1917, the actress Mimí Derba and the producer Enrique Rosas established the Azteca Film Company and produced five films in that one year. Germán Camus built Ediciones Camus S.A. in 1919, and the Estudios Chapultepec opened in 1922. Tomás Pérez Torrent, "The Studio," in *Mexican Cinema,* ed. Paulo Antonio Paranaguá, trans. Ana M. López (London: British Film Institute, 1995), 134.

10. Jorge Negrete, Pedro Infante, and Sara García were the first personalities to rise to the top.

11. Ortega Colunga, "Frente a mi cámara," *Hoy,* June 5, 1943, 70.

12. Carlos Monsiváis, "Dolores del Río: The Face as an Institution," in *Mexican Postcards,* trans. John Kraniauskas (London: Verso, 1997), 81.

13. Ignacio Taibo I attributes del Río's transformation to the "profound friendship" of Fernández, the screenwriter Mauricio Magdaleno, the actor Pedro Armendáriz, and the cinematographer Gabriel Figueroa. "Las estrellas en Mexico," 89.

14. According to Aurelio de los Reyes and García Rojas, Fernández and del Río were involved in an affair that was a "proclaimed secret" in Mexico, an affair upon which del Río "imposed the most absolute of discretions." These authors also suggest that the film was, for Fernández, somewhat autobiographical in its account of a relationship between two lovers of different social classes. Aurelio de los Reyes and García Rojas, *Dolores del Río* (Mexico City: Grupo Condumex, 1996), 97.

15. Héctor Aguilar Camín and Lorenzo Meyer, *In the Shadow of the Mexican Revolution: Contemporary Mexican History, 1910–1989* (Austin: University of Texas Press, 1993), 159. According to Mexican historians Camín and Meyer, after 1940 the idea that "the true Mexico was the one that had not yet appeared and was to be conquered in the future [was] an ideological leap of crucial importance" for contemporary Mexican political and economic reform (189).

16. Quoted in ibid., 161.

17. See Jean Franco's analysis of *Enamorada* for another discussion of how Mexican cinema in the 1940s mediated the "ideological problem" of the post-Revolution Mexican family. Jean Franco, *Plotting Women: Gender and Representation in Mexico* (New York: Columbia University Press, 1989), 148–52.

18. According to Monsiváis, after 1935 Mexican cinema transformed the Revolution "into a nationalist spectacle filled with trains, *soldaderas,* executions, horse cavalcades, cannons, admirable deaths on the portals of Progress, and an indifference to bullets as a sign of faith in the supernatural power of reified historical figures." Monsiváis, "Mythologies," 119.

19. Ana M. López, "Celluloid Tears: Melodrama in the 'Old' Mexican Cinema," *Iris* 13 (summer 1991): 38–39.

20. Franco, *Plotting Women*, 148.

21. De los Reyes and Rojas, *Dolores del Río*, 97.

22. Salvador L. de Ortigosa Jr., "Ultimos estreños," *Hoy*, May 8, 1943, 74.

23. De los Reyes and Rojas, *Dolores del Río*, 93.

24. Ramón, *Dolores del Río*, 2:17.

25. Ibid. Some critics were not so admiring. One columnist found the "development of the film to be quite slow and that, in reality, in the first seven or eight scenes nothing much happens on the screen." De Ortigosa, "Ultimos estreños," 74.

26. Del Río was by no means the most popular Hollywood star in Mexico. She never appeared as regularly as such American actresses as Deanna Durbin, Ginger Rogers, Shirley Temple, Joan Crawford, Carole Lombard, and Bette Davis. In general, throughout the 1930s and 1940s, Mexican newspapers and weekly magazines featured more columns on Hollywood films and stars than they did on Mexican cinema.

27. Despite the increase in Mexican film production, only 6.5 percent of the films that premiered in Mexico City in the 1930s were Mexican. Eduardo de la Vega Alfaro, "Origins, Development and Crisis of the Sound Cinema (1929–64)," in *Mexican Cinema*, ed. Paulo Antonio Paranaguá, trans. Ana M. López (London: British Film Institute, 1995), 84.

28. Howard F. Cline, *Mexico: Revolution to Evolution: 1940–1960* (New York: Oxford University Press, 1963), 124.

29. In 1930 about 6.9 percent of women in Mexico were considered part of the national labor force. Between 1940 and 1950 the percentage of women in the labor force doubled. Morris Singer, *Growth, Equality, and the Mexican Experience*, Latin American Monograph 16 (Austin: Institute of Latin American Studies, University of Texas, 1969), 85.

30. The formation of Mexican nationalism was not unique in this sense. Benedict Anderson writes that "nation-ness is assimilated to skin-colour, gender, parentage, and birth-era—all those things one cannot help." Benedict Anderson, *Imagined Communities: Reflections on the Origin and Spread of Nationalism* (London: Verso, 1983), 131.

31. Unlike the British colonialists of North America, who did not intermarry with the native population, the Spanish did so in great numbers. By the time of the Mexican Revolution, most Mexicans could trace their ancestry to various combinations of European, Indian, and African blood.

32. Aguirre Beltrán argues that "indigenism, basing itself on the mestizo status of the country's population and on the arrogation of the indigenous past, rationalizes the fight which it believes it has to impose a single way out to the Indian: Mexican nationality." Gonzalo Aguirre Beltrán, "El indigenismo y su contribución a la idea de nacionalidad," *América indígena* 29, no. 2 (1969): 404.

33. For an analysis of the Mexican and foreign aesthetic influences on the films of Fernández and his longtime cinematographer, see Charles Ramirez Berg,

"Figueroa's Skies and Oblique Perspective: Notes on the Development of the Classical Mexican Style," *Spectator* 13, no. 1 (1992): 23–38.

34. For a sustained discussion of the historical and cultural foundation of this polarity and of its presentation in Mexican cinema, see Joanne Hershfield, *Mexican Cinema/Mexican Woman, 1940–1950* (Tucson: University of Arizona Press, 1996).

35. Gustavo García credits Figueroa for the "syndrome of Dolores del Río" (responsable del sindrome Dolores del Río). Gustavo García, *La década perdida: Imagen 24 x 1* (Mexico City: Universidad Autonoma Metropolitana, 1986), 26.

36. However, as I have noted elsewhere, Eisenstein's film was itself motivated by exposure to Mexican theater and art before he even arrived in Mexico. In *Immoral Memories: An Autobiography,* trans. Herbert Marshall (Boston: Houghton Mifflin, 1983), Eisenstein writes, "It is here in tierra caliente (burning earth) that I come to know the fantastic structure of prelogical, sensuous thinking—not only from the pages of anthropological investigations, but from daily communion with those descendants of the Aztecs and Toltecs, Mayas, or Huichole who have managed to carry unharmed through the ages that meandering thought" (211). See Joanne Hershfield, "Paradise Regained: Eisenstein's *Que viva México!* as Ethnography," in *Documenting the Documentary,* ed. Barry Grant and Jeannette Sloniowski (Detroit, Mich.: Wayne State University Press, 1998).

37. Although he never completed the project, a number of different films were made from the considerable footage the director shipped backed to the United States for processing. The processed dailies initially remained with the Sinclairs. After their final break with Eisenstein, they sold much of the footage to various people in an attempt to recoup their losses. With this footage, Sol Lesser made two films, *Thunder over Mexico* and *Death Day* (both 1933); a number of ethnographic films were made by the French company Pathé; and Marie Seton produced a short and incomplete film called *Time in the Sun* (1939).

38. Ramirez Berg, "Figueroa's Skies."

39. Aurelio de los Reyes, *Medio siglo de cine Mexicano (1896–1947)* (Mexico City: Editorial Trillas, 1987), 196–97.

40. Marcia Landy, *Cinematic Uses of the Past* (Minneapolis: University of Minnesota Press, 1996), 7, 8.

41. Ibid., 1.

42. Ibid.

43. Quoted in Jackie Stacey, *Star Gazing: Hollywood Cinema and Female Spectatorship* (London: Routledge, 1994), 126. For Stacey, what is significant is the "range of identifications" that are processed through mechanisms of fantasy and material practice (see especially chap. 5).

44. For a discussion of the *cabaretera* films of the 1940s, see Hershfield, *Mexican Cinema/Mexican Woman,* chap. 4.

45. Carlos Monsiváis, "Santa: El cine naturalista," in *Anuario 1965* (Departamento de Actividades Cinematográficas) (Mexico City: UNAM, 1966); quoted in de los Reyes, *Medio siglo de cine Mexicano,* 123.

46. David Ramón recounts the strange history behind the production of *La selva de fuego*. Antonio Momplet, a Spanish émigré, discussed with Clasa the possibility of directing del Río in *Vértigo*, a film about a woman who, when quite young, married a much older man. Upon his death, she inherits his money and property. The widow subsequently falls in love with her daughter's fiancé. At the same time, Clasa planned to produce *La selva de fuego*, in which Fernando de Fuentes would direct María Félix. Through a mix-up, del Río received a copy of the *La selva de fuego* script while the studio sent Félix the screenplay for *Vértigo*. When the executives at Clasa realized the mistake and approached the two stars, both women refused to exchange their scripts. Ramón, *Dolores del Río*, 2:25.

47. Revueltas's script was based on the same American novel as was the Hollywood film *The Dark Mirror*, starring Olivia de Havilland, released the same year. Ariel Zúñega discusses the similarities and differences between *La otra* and *The Dark Mirror* in his essay "Roberto Galvadón," in *Mexican Cinema*, ed. Paulo Antonio Paranaguá, trans. Ana M. López (London: British Film Institute, 1995).

48. Monsiváis, "Dolores del Río," 87.

49. García, *La década perdida*, 30–44.

50. Ibid., 34.

51. Ibid., 88.

52. De la Vega Alfaro, "Origins, Development and Crisis," 88.

53. García, *La década perdida*, 88–89.

54. Ibid., 22.

55. Monsiváis, "Mythologies," 119.

56. According to David Ramón, the Mexican public imagined a rivalry between the two stars and "invented histories" to support their conviction. Ramón, *Dolores del Río*, 2:25. In 1945, Félix commanded, on the average, 150,000 pesos per film. Del Río received 50,000 pesos plus 15 percent of the film's gross. Emilio García Riera, *Historia documental del cine Mexicano: Época sonora*, vol. 3, *1945–1948* (Mexico City: Ediciones Era, 1969), 9.

57. *Soldaderas*, or female "soldiers," worked as cooks and nurses, and many even carried and used weapons during the Mexican Revolution. These women became famous in legends, in songs, and in the movies as La Adelita, La Valentina, La Cucaracha, and Juana Gallo. For a critical discussion of *soldaderas*, see Elizabeth Salas, *Soldaderas in the Mexican Military: Myth and History* (Austin: University of Texas Press, 1990).

58. In Carmen Huaco-Nuzam's words, "Landeta anticipated the multiple concerns of modern feminism—the articulation of oppression across gender, race, and class." Carmen Huaco-Nuzam, "Matilde Landeta," *Screen* 28, no. 4 (1987): 105.

59. Monsiváis, "Mythologies," 121.

60. Ilene V. O'Malley, *The Myth of the Revolution: Hero Cults and the Institutionalization of the Mexican State, 1920–1940* (Westport, Conn.: Greenwood, 1986), 7.

61. Monsiváis, "Dolores del Río," 82.

## 5. Mexico Is a State of Mind

The title of this chapter comes from Graham Greene, *Another Mexico* (New York: Viking, 1939), 272.

1. The novel, published in 1940, was originally titled *The Labyrinthine Ways*.

2. "The New Pictures," *Time*, December 1, 1947, 105; "The Last Priest," *Newsweek*, January 12, 1948, 78; John McCarthy, "Up from the Border," *New Yorker*, December 27, 1947, 38.

3. Greene made the trip to Mexico in the employ of a major British Catholic publishing house, Sheed and Ward.

4. Mary Louise Pratt, *Imperial Eyes: Travel Writing and Transculturation* (London: Routledge, 1992), 75. In an interesting earlier essay, Pratt examines the function of "the personal narrative" in ethnographic writing (for example, the published diaries of Malinowski). In the professional, academic world, "the formal ethnography is the one that counts as professional capital and as an authoritative representation; the personal narratives are often deemed self-indulgent, trivial, or heretical." Mary Louise Pratt, "Fieldwork in Common Places," in *Writing Culture: The Poetics and Politics of Ethnography*, ed. James Clifford and George E. Marcus (Berkeley: University of California Press, 1986), 31.

5. W. J. West, *The Quest for Graham Greene* (London: Weidenfeld & Nicolson, 1997), xiv. West also quotes from another biography by Norman Sherry: "Novels declare themselves as fictions not as personal histories, though they mine the personal terrain. Greene always felt that so long as he presented his intimate experiences as fictions his secrets would remain unrecognized." Norman Sherry, *The Life of Graham Greene*, vol. 2, *1939–55* (New York: Viking, 1995), 234.

6. Greene, *Another Mexico*, 38.

7. Ibid, 240.

8. Ibid., 48.

9. James Clifford, *The Predicament of Culture: Twentieth-Century Ethnography, Literature, and Art* (Cambridge: Harvard University Press, 1988), 10.

10. Greene, *Another Mexico*, 8, 9.

11. Ibid., 186. Greene's travelogue offers no critical explanation or analysis of this revolt. Instead, *Another Mexico* inserts itself into a long line of imperialist "autobiographies" that invoke the genre of the "personal narrative." See Pratt's discussion of Alexander von Humboldt's writings. According to Pratt, von Humboldt's narrative of his expedition around the South American continent at the end of the eighteenth century "laid down the lines for the ideological reinvention of South America." *Imperial Eyes*, 112.

12. Jean Meyer, *The Cristero Rebellion: The Mexican People between Church and State, 1926–1929* (London: Cambridge University Press, 1976), 187. In Meyer's estimation, the Cristero Revolt was not politically motivated; rather it was inspired by spiritual and cultural concerns. The peasants of Jalisco did not take up arms only because of their opposition to land reforms but "because the Revolution was

trying to take the priest away from them" (186). In *Another Mexico,* Greene also describes the Cristero Revolt as a battle over "the soul of the Indian" (10).

13. J. A. Place, *Non-Western Films of John Ford* (New York: Citadel, 1979), 263–64. See also Charles Ramirez Berg, "Figueroa's Skies and Oblique Perspective: Notes on the Development of the Classical Mexican Style," *Spectator* 13, no. 1 (1992): 23–38.

14. Carlos Monsiváis finds that "Fernández and Ford both organize their sequences in an operatic delirium, and Figueroa finds the scenes and frames that correspond to the spiritual temper of the characters." Carlos Monsiváis, "Establishing Point of View," in *Artes de Mexico: El arte de Gabriel Figueroa* (Mexico City: Libro Trimestral, 1988), 94.

15. Tag Gallagher, *John Ford: The Man and His Films* (Berkeley: University of California Press, 1986), 234.

16. Ibid., 51–53. According to Figueroa, his cinematography was also influenced by German expressionism of the 1920s, "where the use of composition, painted curtains and large shadows gave incredible force to the image." Quoted in Margarita de Orellana, "Words Regarding Images: An Interview with Gabriel Figueroa," in *Artes de Mexico: El arte de Gabriel Figueroa* (Mexico City: Libro Trimestral, 1988), 92.

17. Gallagher, *John Ford,* 53.

18. Gallagher separates Murnau's expressionism (with a small *e*) from German Expressionism, saying that the former "is concerned with the subjective or poetic aspect of things, and is virtually equivalent to 'style.' 'Subjectivity' implies meaning . . . 'reality,' on the other hand is by definition meaningless and emotionless; thus filmic realism is, in theory, styleless" (ibid., 51).

19. Ibid., 53.

20. I have argued that, for Eisenstein, Mexico also functioned as the ground for an exploration of the self. See Joanne Hershfield, "Paradise Regained: Eisenstein's *Que viva México!* as Ethnography," in *Documenting the Documentary,* ed. Barry Grant and Jeannette Sloniowski (Detroit, Mich.: Wayne State University Press, 1998).

21. Gallagher, *John Ford,* 50.

22. Ibid., 235.

23. Richard Slotkin, *Gunfighter Nation: The Myth of the Frontier in Twentieth-Century America* (New York: Atheneum, 1992), 418.

24. For a history and analysis of U.S. intellectual, artistic, and popular response to the Mexican Revolution, see John A. Britton, *Revolution and Ideology: Images of the Mexican Revolution in the United States* (Lexington: University Press of Kentucky, 1995).

25. Gallagher, *John Ford,* 234 n.

26. Judith Mayne, *Private Novels, Public Films* (Athens: University of Georgia Press, 1988), 101.

27. Rey Chow, *Primitive Passions: Visuality, Sexuality, Ethnography, and Contemporary Chinese Cinema* (New York: Columbia University Press, 1995), 182.

28. Tejaswini Niranjana, *Siting Translation: History, Post-Structuralism, and the Colonial Context* (Berkeley: University of California Press, 1992), 163.

29. Ibid., 3.

30. Similarly, in MGM's *Viva Villa!* (1934, Jack Conway), the Mexican Revolution emerges as a populist allegory about an individual's heroic commitment to democratic values. As discussed earlier, Mexican viewers condemned *Viva Villa!* for propagating Hollywood's classical race and class stereotypes.

31. Obviously, I am indebted to Pratt's work in *Imperial Eyes*, for her exploration of how "travel and exploration writing *produced* 'the rest of the world' for European readerships" (5).

32. Quentin Falk, *Travels in Greeneland: The Cinema of Graham Greene* (London: Quartet, 1984), 98–99.

33. Quoted in ibid., 99.

34. Slotkin, *Gunfighter Nation*, 412.

35. By the 1940s, American attitudes about Mexicans and other ethnic groups had been affected by changing social and political circumstances, including demographic changes due to migration and immigration, the growth in educational opportunities and experiences of the American public, and an increase in numbers and an expansion across the United States of Spanish-speaking immigrants. At the same time, deeply felt popular understandings of racial differences persisted in American cultural beliefs, attitudes, and practices. Among U.S. respondents to a poll conducted by the Office of Public Opinion in 1949, 40 to 50 percent selected the adjectives "dark-skinned," "quick-tempered," "emotional," "superstitious," "backward," "lazy," "ignorant," and "suspicious" to describe people from Latin America. Cited in Frederick B. Pike, *The United States and Latin America: Myths and Stereotypes of Civilization and Nature* (Austin: University of Texas Press, 1992), 291–92.

36. Ten "unfriendly witnesses" who declined to cooperate with the committee were imprisoned. Four years later, in the midst of vicious Cold War anticommunist rhetoric and politics, HUAC called another two hundred Hollywood "witnesses." Those who refused to "name names" were officially blacklisted by the industry in the infamous "Waldorf Statement." This statement, issued jointly by the MPAA and the Association of Motion Picture Producers, stated that the industry would not "knowingly employ a Communist or member of any party or group which advocates the overthrow of the government of the United States by force or by illegal or unconstitutional methods." See Gordon Kahn, *Hollywood on Trial: The Story of the Ten Who Were Indicted* (New York: Boni & Gaer, 1948); Larry Ceplair and Steven Englund, *The Inquisition in Hollywood: Politics in the Film Community, 1930–1960* (New York: Doubleday, 1980).

37. Aurelio de los Reyes and García Rojas, *Dolores del Río* (Mexico City: Grupo Condumex, 1996), 117.

38. Hobe, *Variety*, November 5, 1947, 8.

39. Bosley Crowther, *New York Times*, December 26, 1947. Thirty years latter,

critics still commented on the double themes of politics and religion in *The Fugitive*. Andrew Sarris, in *The John Ford Movie Mystery* (Bloomington: Indiana University Press, 1975), writes that Ford's film is a "solidly pro-Catholic picture . . . [and] a bad work of art, tacky, unreal, and pretentious" (120).

40. "Movies: the Wreckers," *New Republic*, December 29, 1947, 34.

41. McCarthy, "Up from the Border," 38.

42. The film was originally intended to be a documentary, an educational film aimed at Mexico's huge and diverse illiterate population, but was transformed into a narrative film when Strand and Zinnemann were brought in.

43. Fred Zinnemann, *An Autobiography: A Life in the Movies* (New York: Charles Scribner's Sons, 1992), 31.

44. Carlos Monsiváis, "Mythologies," in *Mexican Cinema*, ed. Paulo Antonio Paranagua, trans. Ana M. López (London: British Film Institute, 1995), 119.

45. Edward W. Said, *Orientalism* (New York: Vintage, 1979), 166.

46. Ibid., 168–69.

47. For an analysis of Hollywood cinema as ethnographic cinema, see Fatimah Tobing Rony, *The Third Eye: Race, Cinema, and Ethnographic Spectacle* (Durham, N.C.: Duke University Press, 1996). See also the chapter titled "Film as Ethnography; or, Translation between Cultures in the Postcolonial World" in Chow, *Primitive Passions*. Chow looks at autoethnographic practices, at postcolonial subjects "who have, in the postcolonial age, taken up the active task of ethnographizing their own cultures" (180). Specifically, she considers Chinese filmmakers who have "translated" China into film for non-Chinese audiences.

48. Niranjana, *Siting Translation*, 8.

## 6. Race on the Range

1. According to de los Reyes and Rojas, 20th Century Fox offered del Río a role in *Flaming Star* as part of a public relations ploy. Mexico had prohibited the exhibition of any of Presley's films following a public statement the singer made in 1959 that one of the last things he would ever think of doing would be to kiss a Mexican woman. See Aurelio de los Reyes and García Rojas, *Dolores del Río* (Mexico City: Grupo Condumex, 1996), 117. Apparently, Fox producers felt that the presence of del Río opposite Presley would mitigate the antagonism of the Mexican public.

2. Del Río appeared in a number of U.S. dramatic television shows in the 1950s and 1960s, including *Schlitz Playhouse, U.S. Steel Hour, The Man Who Bought Paradise, I Spy*, and *Branded*.

3. Kathy Peiss, *Hope in a Jar: The Making of America's Beauty Culture* (New York: Henry Holt, 1998), 248. E. Ann Kaplan notes how remarkable it is that "concepts of menopausal women have somehow remained unchanged in the cultural unconsciousness, despite changes that feminism(s) have managed to produce regarding other kinds of female stereotypes." E. Ann Kaplan, *Looking for the Other: Feminism, Film, and the Imperial Gaze* (New York: Routledge, 1997), 269.

4. I have adapted the term *nonwhite woman-structure* from Annette Kuhn's explanation of the "woman structure." As Kuhn explains the term, "no longer is 'woman' regarded as a concrete gendered human being . . . 'she' becomes, on the contrary, a structure governing the organization of story and plot in a narrative or group of narratives." Annette Kuhn, *Women's Pictures: Feminism and Cinema* (London: Verso, 1993), 32.

5. According to Todd Gitlin, "Rock 'n' roll was [black] rhythm and blues whitened. . . . [It] brought the pulse of R&B to places where blacks themselves never dreamed of going; at the same time it blanched the music." It was this phenomenon, in fact, that produced Elvis Presley, lauded in rock-and-roll history as "the white boy with the black beat." Todd Gitlin, *The Sixties: Years of Hope, Days of Rage* (Toronto: Bantam, 1987), 38.

6. Peggy Pascoe, "Miscegenation Law, Court Cases, and Ideologies of 'Race' in Twentieth-Century America," *Journal of American History* 83 (June 1996): 48. See also Michael Omi and Howard Winant, *Racial Formation in the United States: From the 1960s to the 1990s,* 2d ed. (New York: Routledge, 1994), 57. As Omi and Winant note, regardless of the "official" moral and political policy, there coexist numerous projects across the "political spectrum of racial formation," from biologist views of white supremacy to promotions and celebrations of racial difference (58). For a discussion of this spectrum, see also Kimberle Crenshaw, "Race, Reform, and Retrenchment: Transformation and Legitimation in Anti-discrimination Law," in *Critical Race Theory: The Key Writings That Formed the Movement,* edited by Kimberle Crenshaw, Neil Gotanda, Garry Peller, and Kendall Thomas (New York: New Press, 1995).

7. For Benedict Anderson, nineteenth-century American "imaginings" of racial fraternity in popular and epic narrative constructions "show as clearly as anything else that nationalism" during that moment "represented a new form of consciousness—a consciousness that arose when it was no longer possible to experience the nation as new." Because the formation of a national identity "can not be remembered, [it] must be narrated." Benedict Anderson, *Imagined Communities: Reflections on the Origin and Spread of Nationalism,* rev. ed. (London: Verso, 1991), 203–4. Anderson cites examples such as James Fenimore Cooper's *The Pathfinder,* Herman Melville's *Moby Dick,* and Mark Twain's *Huckleberry Finn.* Cooper, for example, published *The Pathfinder,* a novel that celebrates the friendship between a white man and an Indian chief in 1840, "in the midst of a brutal eight-year war against the Seminoles of Florida." However, he set the story almost a decade earlier and situated both men as "Americans," fighting in the service of George III "for survival—against the French" (202–3).

8. Sal Mineo had earlier played a Chicano character in *Giant* (1956, George Stevens).

9. John D'Emilio and Estelle B. Freedman, *Intimate Matters: A History of Sexuality in America* (New York: Harper & Row, 1988), 87.

10. William Cronon, George Miles, and Jay Gitlin, "Becoming West: Toward a

New Meaning for Western History," in *Under an Open Sky: Rethinking America's Western Past,* ed. William Cronon, George Miles, and Jay Gitlin (New York: W. W. Norton, 1992), 21.

11. Ibid. 6.

12. See Frederick Jackson Turner, "The Significance of the Frontier in American History" (originally published in *Annual Report of the American Historical Association for the Year 1893* [Washington, D.C., 1894]), in *Rereading Frederick Jackson Turner: "The Significance of the Frontier in American History" and Other Essays* (New York: Henry Holt, 1994). Turner writes that "the wilderness masters the colonist. It finds him a European in dress, industries, tools, modes of travel, and thought. It takes him from the railroad car and puts him in the birch canoe. It strips off the garments of civilization and arrays him in the hunting shirt and the moccasin. . . . Little by little he transforms the wilderness, but the outcome is not the old Europe. . . . The fact is, that here is a new product that is American" (33–34). For a contemporary review of the classical paradigm of Western expansion, see Patricia Nelson Limerick, *The Legacy of Conquest: The Unbroken Past of the American West* (New York: W. W. Norton, 1987).

13. "Not white" is a trope of whiteness. Richard Dyer outlines "a whole series of tropes of whiteness" that proceed from the frontier myth. According to Dyer, the landscape itself "calls forth qualities of character" that are racially represented. Richard Dyer, *White* (London: Routledge, 1997), 34.

14. Ann Fabian, "History for the Masses: Commercializing the Western Past," in *Under an Open Sky: Rethinking America's Western Past,* ed. William Cronon, George Miles, and Jay Gitlin (New York: W. W. Norton, 1992), 223.

15. For a discussion of the intersection of these two discourses in popular American historiography, see Rick Worland and Edward Countryman, "The New Western American Historiography and the Emergence of the New American Westerns," in *Back in the Saddle Again: New Essays on the Western,* ed. Edward Buscombe and Roberta E. Pearson (London: British Film Institute, 1998). According to Worland and Countryman, "for the most part, Cody's framework of understanding has ruled, not Turner's" (183).

16. Although historians of the 1950s and 1960s were abandoning Turner's thesis and traditional frontier historiography because it was "racist, sexist, and imperialist. . . . it remained a much-beloved subject for ordinary Americans." Cronon et al., "Becoming West," 4.

17. Frederick Jackson Turner, *The Frontier in American History* (New York: Holt, Rinehart & Winston, 1920), 1; quoted in ibid., 6. Despite their disagreements with some of Turner's assumptions, contemporary scholars of the west generally agree with this thesis.

18. As Fabian notes, "Tales of violence and bloodshed continued to serve the commercial ends of those engaged in the marketing of the West." "History for the Masses," 228.

19. In a recent two-part essay in the *New Yorker* about the legend of Billy the

Kid, Fintan O'Toole offers up another version of the American West. O'Toole argues that "before he was William Bonney, even before he was Kid Antrim or Henry Antrim or any of the other names he used, he was Henry McCarty . . . born, possibly in County Limerick [Ireland], but more probably in the Irish slums of New York." According to the official legend, Billy initially made his reputation killing Indians and Mexicans. According to O'Toole, however, the Kid was involved in a different kind of racial war in New Mexico, Arizona, and Northern Mexico: an economic and "vicious sectarian battle fought between Irish Catholics and British Protestants." Fintan O'Toole, *New Yorker*, December 28, 1998, and January 4, 1999.

20. Limerick, *The Legacy of Conquest*, 260.

21. See Richard Abel, "'Our Country'/Whose Country? The 'Americanization' Project of Early Westerns," in *Back in the Saddle Again: New Essays on the Western*, ed. Edward Buscombe and Roberta E. Pearson (London: British Film Institute, 1998).

22. Richard Slotkin, *Gunfighter Nation: The Myth of the Frontier in Twentieth-Century America* (New York: Atheneum, 1992), 248.

23. Ibid., 243.

24. Ibid., 247–48.

25. Lee Clark Mitchell, *Westerns: Making the Man in Fiction and Film* (Chicago: University of Chicago Press, 1994), 3.

26. *Hollywood Reporter*, December 1, 1960, 3.

27. Bosley Crowther, *New York Times*, December 24, 1964.

28. "Indian Exodus," *Time*, January 8, 1965, 54.

29. Brendan Gill, "Current Cinema," *New Yorker*, January 2, 1965, 65.

30. Stanley Kauffmann, "No Ford in Our Future," *New Republic*, January 23, 1965, 36.

31. Slotkin, *Gunfighter Nation*, 629.

32. Michael Coyne, *The Crowded Prairie: American National Identity in the Hollywood Western* (New York: St. Martin's Press, 1997), 123. Coyne also suggests that the film "even evokes the recently slain Kennedy, as Secretary of the Interior Carl Schurz (Edward G. Robinson) gazes wistfully at a portrait of Lincoln and asks the martyred president, 'Old friend—what would you do?'" (123).

33. Michael Rogin diagrams the link between the two historical manifestations of national racial practices, writing that "the expropriation of Indian land and the exploitation of black labor lie at the root not only of America's economic development, but of its political conflicts and cultural identity as well." Michael P. Rogin, "Kiss Me Deadly: Communism, Motherhood, and Cold War Memories," *Representations* 6 (1984): 1.

34. For a thoughtful critique of the argument that pro-Indian westerns of the 1960s are "allegories" of the civil rights movement, see Steve Neales, "Vanishing Americans: Racial and Ethnic Issues in the Interpretation and Context of Post-War 'Pro-Indian' Westerns," in *Back in the Saddle Again: New Essays on the Western*, ed. Edward Buscombe and Roberta E. Pearson (London: British Film Institute, 1998).

35. Marcia Landy, *Film, Politics, and Gramsci* (Minneapolis: University of Minnesota Press, 1996), 7–8.

36. Anderson, *Imagined Communities,* 205.

37. Virginia Wright Wexman, "The Family on the Land: Race and Nationhood in Silent Westerns," in *The Birth of Whiteness: Race and the Emergence of U.S. Cinema,* ed. Daniel Bernardi (New Brunswick, N.J.: Rutgers University Press, 1996), 132. A number of very early silent westerns contemplated interracial marriage, including *'Twixt Love and Duty* (1908), *The Kentuckian* (1908), and *Comata, the Sioux* (1909). See Allen L. Woll, *The Latin Image in American Film* (Los Angeles: UCLA Latin American Center Publications, 1980), xvii.

38. The Indian male functioned in the same way black men functioned in white American imagination. His was an uncontrolled sexuality whose strongest erotic desire was to rape white women.

39. John G. Cawelti, *The Six-Gun Mystique* (Bowling Green, Ohio: Bowling Green State University Press, 1971), 47.

40. D'Emilio and Freedman, *Intimate Matters,* 87. Despite these prejudices, D'Emilio and Freedman note that intermarriage between white men and Indian or Mexican women occurred frequently (90).

41. Dyer, *White,* 36.

42. A number of other films made during this period—*The Magnificent Seven* (1960), *One-Eyed Jacks* (1961), *Rio Conchos* (1964), *100 Rifles* (1969), and *The Wild Bunch* (1969)—also have been lauded for their liberalist sensibilities in regard to the treatment of Native Americans and thus for "radically" transforming the genre.

43. In *The Six-Gun Mystique,* Cawelti notes that "in 1959, eight of the top ten shows on television, as measured by Nielsen ratings, were Westerns and thirty of the prime-time shows were horse operas" (2). By 1970, however, the television western was in decline. According to Edward Buscombe, the decline was not due to "a fall in popularity"; rather, the western was a "casualty of demographics." Television westerns were found to appeal to juveniles and to rural and lower-class segments of the population. "Since television needed to sell advertising time, not programmes, it soon realized that it could do better with shows which appealed to the more affluent." Edward Buscombe, ed., *The BFI Companion to the Western* (London: British Film Institute, 1988), 47.

44. Slotkin, *Gunfighter Nation,* 377. Coyne, however, points out that although *Broken Arrow* "was influential in reshaping Hollywood's representation of the Indian, a genre which thrived on violence could reap only limited rewards from a pacifist premise." *The Crowded Prairie,* 70.

45. Cawelti, *The Six-Gun Mystique,* 37–38.

46. For a discussion of the links between the "imperial film" and the western, see Ella Shohat and Robert Stam's discussion of "the imperial imaginary" in *Unthinking Eurocentrism: Multiculturalism and the Media* (London: Routledge, 1994), 100–31.

47. Ibid., 156.

48. Laura Mulvey, "Pandora: Topographies of the Mask and Curiosity," in *Sexuality and Space,* ed. Beatriz Columina (Princeton, N.J.: Princeton Architectural Press, 1992), 56.

49. Kuhn, *Women's Pictures,* 34–35.

50. Mary Ann Doane, "Dark Continents: Epistemologies of Racial and Sexual Difference in Psychoanalysis and the Cinema," in *Femmes Fatales: Feminism, Film Theory, Psychoanalysis* (London: Routledge, 1991), 229.

51. Ibid., 230.

Conclusion

1. Richard Dyer, "Charisma," in *Stardom: Industry of Desire,* ed. Christine Gledhill (London: Routledge, 1991), 58.

2. Ed Guerrero, *Framing Blackness: The African American Image in Film* (Philadelphia: Temple University Press, 1993), 157.

3. These black-and-white "buddy" films, one of the most successful genres of the crossover films, can be seen as homoerotic interracial romances. Guerrero notes, however, that because "of his tremendous 'crossover' appeal," in the *Beverly Hills Cop* series, Murphy "was able to renegotiate the terms of the buddy formula, making it his exclusive star vehicle" (ibid., 132). Murphy has become, in other words, what Tom Schatz refers to as a "mega" star. Schatz argues that, because of the high costs and profit potential of motion picture production in the 1990s, the "values" of the most marketable stars have skyrocketed to the point where some "mega" stars have become "not only genres but franchises unto themselves." Thomas Schatz, "The New Hollywood," in *Film Theory Goes to the Movies,* ed. Jim Collins, Hilary Radner, and Ava Preacher Collins (New York: Routledge, 1993), 31.

4. Sharon Willis, *High Contrast: Race and Gender in Contemporary Hollywood Film* (Durham, N.C.: Duke University Press, 1997), 170.

5. Ed Guerrero, "Spike Lee and the Fever in the Racial Jungle," in *Film Theory Goes to the Movies,* ed. Jim Collins, Hilary Radner, and Ava Preacher Collins (New York: Routledge, 1993), 174.

6. Chon A. Noriega marks the release of Luis Valdez's *La Bamba* in 1987 as the year "Chicano cinema entered into the so-called mainstream." Chon A. Noriega, "Introduction," in *Chicanos and Film: Representation and Resistance,* ed. Chon A. Noriega (Minneapolis: University of Minnesota Press, 1992), xi. *La Bamba* has been received by Chicana/o scholars in diverse ways. Victor Fuentes argues that the film's representations of Chicana/os "has a strong appeal for the latino/a viewer." He finds "despite the stereotype of a number of the characters in the film," the farmworker family in Valdez's film is "accurately represented, as far as customs, gestures, feelings, and language." Victor Fuentes, "Chicano Cinema: A Dialectic between Voices and Images of the Autonomous Discourse versus Those of the Dominant," also in *Chicanos and Film,* 212.

7. Fuentes, "Chicano Cinema," 213.

8. Rosa Linda Fregoso, *The Bronze Screen: Chicana and Chicano Film Culture* (Minneapolis: University of Minnesota Press, 1993), 93–94.

9. Ibid., 54.

10. Review of *Out of Sight, Raleigh (N.C.) News and Observer,* March 17, 1998, 3.

11. Eric Gutierrez, "In the Game at Last," *Los Angeles Times,* March 16, 1997.

12. Ibid.

13. Bordwell, Thompson, and Staiger have argued that the "classical Hollywood style" persists in the films of the post-1960s "New Hollywood." They insist that stylistically, narratively, and generically, contemporary Hollywood films "remain within classical boundaries." David Bordwell, Kristen Thompson, and Janet Staiger, *The Classical Hollywood Cinema: Film Style and Mode of Production to 1960* (New York: Columbia University Press, 1985), 373–77.

14. Ed Guerrero, "The Black Image in Protective Custody: Hollywood's Biracial Buddy Films of the Eighties," in *Black American Cinema,* ed. Manthia Diawara (New York: Routledge, 1993), 237.

15. Judith Mayne, *Cinema and Spectatorship* (London: Routledge, 1993), 97.

16. Carol Clover, "Her Body, Himself: Gender in the Slasher Film," in *Dread of Difference: Gender and the Horror Film,* ed. Barry K. Grant (Austin: University of Texas Press, 1996), 96.

17. Jackie Stacey, *Star Gazing: Hollywood Cinema and Female Spectatorship* (London: Routledge, 1994), 174–75.

# Bibliography

Abel, Richard. "'Our Country'/Whose Country? The 'Americanization' Project of Early Westerns." In *Back in the Saddle Again: New Essays on the Western*, edited by Edward Buscombe and Roberta E. Pearson London: British Film Institute, 1998.

Alexander, Karen. "Fatal Beauties: Black Women in Hollywood." In *Stardom: Industry of Desire*, edited by Christine Gledhill. London: Routledge, 1991.

Anderson, Benedict. *Imagined Communities: Reflections on the Origin and Spread of Nationalism.* London: Verso, 1983.

Augusto, Sérgio. "Hollywood Looks at Brazil: From Carmen Miranda to *Moonraker*." In *Brazilian Cinema*, expanded ed., edited by Randal Johnson and Robert Stam. Berkeley: University of California Press, 1996.

Balibar, Etienne, and Immanuel Wallerstein. *Race, Nation and Class: Ambiguous Identities.* London: Verso, 1994.

Beltrán, Gonzalo Aguirre. "El indigenismo y su contribución a la idea de nacionalidad." *América indígena* 29, no. 2 (1969): 397–406.

Berenstein, Rhona J. "Spectatorship-as-Drag: The Act of Viewing and Classic Horror Cinema." In *Viewing Positions: Ways of Seeing Film*, edited by Linda Williams. New Brunswick, N.J.: Rutgers University Press, 1995.

———. *Attack of the Leading Ladies: Gender, Sexuality, and Spectatorship in Classic Horror Cinema.* New York: Columbia University Press, 1996.

Bergman, Andrew W. *We're in the Money: Depression America and Its Films.* New York: New York University Press, 1971.

Bernardi, Daniel. "The Voice of Whiteness: D. W. Griffith's Biograph Films (1908–1913)." In *The Birth of Whiteness: Race and the Emergence of U.S. Cinema,* edited by Daniel Bernardi. New Brunswick, N.J.: Rutgers University Press, 1996.

Bhabha, Homi K. "The Other Question: Homi K. Bhabha Reconsiders the Stereotype and Colonial Discourse." *Screen* 24, no. 6 (1983).

Black, Gregory D. *Hollywood Censored: Morality Codes, Catholics, and the Movies.* New York: Cambridge University Press, 1994.

Bordwell, David, Kristen Thompson, and Janet Staiger. *The Classical Hollywood Cinema: Film Style and Mode of Production to 1960.* New York: Columbia University Press, 1985.

Britton, Andrew. "Stars and Genre." In *Stardom: Industry of Desire,* edited by Christine Gledhill. London: Routledge, 1991.

Britton, John A. *Revolution and Ideology: Images of the Mexican Revolution in the United States.* Lexington: University Press of Kentucky, 1995.

Bruno, Giuliana. *Streetwalking on a Ruined Map: Cultural Theory and the City Films of Elvira Notari.* Princeton, N.J.: Princeton University Press, 1993.

Camín, Héctor Aguilar, and Lorenzo Meyer. *In the Shadow of the Mexican Revolution: Contemporary Mexican History, 1910–1989.* Austin: University of Texas Press, 1993.

Cawelti, John G. *The Six-Gun Mystique.* Bowling Green, Ohio: Bowling Green State University Press, 1971.

Chow, Rey. *Primitive Passions: Visuality, Sexuality, Ethnography, and Contemporary Chinese Cinema.* New York: Columbia University Press, 1995.

Clifford, James. *The Predicament of Culture: Twentieth-Century Ethnography, Literature, and Art.* Cambridge: Harvard University Press, 1988.

Cline, Howard F. *Mexico: Revolution to Evolution: 1940–1960.* New York: Oxford University Press, 1963.

Couvares, Francis G., ed. *Movie Censorship and American Culture.* Washington, D.C.: Smithsonian Institution Press, 1996.

Cronon, William, George Miles, and Jay Gitlin. "Becoming West: Toward a New Meaning for Western History." In *Under an Open Sky: Rethinking America's*

*Western Past*, edited by William Cronon, George Miles, and Jay Gitlin. New York: W. W. Norton, 1992.

Curry, Ramona. *Too Much of a Good Thing: Mae West as Cultural Icon.* Minneapolis: University of Minnesota Press, 1996.

de Certeau, Michel. *The Writing of History.* New York: Columbia University Press, 1988.

deCordova, Richard. *Picture Personalities: The Emergence of the Star System in America.* Urbana: University of Illinois Press, 1990.

Delpar, Helen. "Goodbye to the Greaser: Mexico, the MPPDA, and Derogatory Films, 1922–1926." *Journal of Popular Film and Television* 12, no. 1 (1984).

D'Emilio, John, and Estelle B. Freedman. *Intimate Matters: A History of Sexuality in America.* New York: Harper & Row, 1988.

Doane, Mary Ann. "Dark Continents: Epistemologies of Racial and Sexual Difference in Psychoanalysis and the Cinema." In *Femmes Fatales: Feminism, Film Theory, Psychoanalysis.* London: Routledge, 1991.

Donahue, Suzanne Mary. *American Film Distribution: The Changing Marketplace.* Ann Arbor, Mich.: UMI Research Press, 1987.

Dumenil, Lynn. *The Modern Temper: American Culture and Society in the 1920s.* New York: Hill & Wang, 1995.

Dyer, Richard. "Entertainment and Utopia." In *Movies and Methods*, vol. 2, edited by Bill Nichols. Berkeley: University of California Press, 1985.

———. "Paul Robeson: Crossing Over." In *Heavenly Bodies: Film Stars and Society.* New York: St. Martin's Press, 1986.

———. "Charisma." In *Stardom: Industry of Desire*, edited by Christine Gledhill. London: Routledge, 1991.

———. *White.* London: Routledge, 1997.

Eckert, Charles. "The Carole Lombard in Macy's Window." *Quarterly Review of Film Studies* 3, no. 1 (1978).

Eco, Umberto. *The Limits of Interpretation.* Bloomington: Indiana University Press, 1990.

Fabian, Ann. "History for the Masses: Commercializing the Western Past," in *Under an Open Sky: Rethinking America's Western Past*, edited by William Cronon, George Miles, and Jay Gitlin. New York: W. W. Norton, 1992.

Falk, Quentin. *Travels in Greeneland: The Cinema of Graham Greene.* London: Quartet, 1984.

Foucault, Michel. *History of Sexuality,* vol. 1, *An Introduction.* New York: Vintage, 1990.

Franco, Jean. *Plotting Women: Gender and Representation in Mexico.* New York: Columbia University Press, 1989.

Fregoso, Rosa Linda. *The Bronze Screen: Chicana and Chicano Film Culture.* Minneapolis: University of Minnesota Press, 1993.

Gallagher, Tag. *John Ford: The Man and His Films.* Berkeley: University of California Press, 1986.

García, Gustavo. *La década perdida: Imagen 24 x 1.* Mexico City: Universidad Autonoma Metropolitana, 1986.

García Riera, Emilio. *El cine Mexicano.* Mexico City: Era, 1963.

———. *Historia documental del cine Mexicano: Época sonora,* vol. 3, *1945–1948.* Mexico City: Era, 1969.

Gilman, Sander L. *Difference and Pathology: Stereotypes of Sexuality, Race and Madness.* Ithaca, N.Y.: Cornell University Press, 1985.

Gilroy, Paul. *There Ain't No Black in the Union Jack.* London: Hutchinson, 1987.

Greene, Graham. *Another Mexico.* New York: Viking, 1939.

Guerrero, Ed. "The Black Image in Protective Custody: Hollywood's Biracial Buddy Films of the Eighties." In *Black American Cinema,* edited by Manthia Diawara. New York: Routledge, 1993.

———. *Framing Blackness: The African American Image in Film.* Philadelphia: Temple University Press, 1993.

———. "Spike Lee and the Fever in the Racial Jungle." In *Film Theory Goes to the Movies,* edited by Jim Collins, Hilary Radner, and Ava Preacher Collins. New York: Routledge, 1993.

Gunning, Tom. *D. W. Griffith and the Origins of American Narrative Film: The Early Years at Biograph.* Urbana: University of Illinois Press, 1994.

Hansen, Miriam. "Early Cinema, Late Cinema: Transformations of the Public Sphere." In *Viewing Positions: Ways of Seeing Film,* edited by Linda Williams. New Brunswick, N.J.: Rutgers University Press, 1995.

Harris, Thomas. "The Building of Popular Images: Grace Kelly and Marilyn Monroe." In *Stardom: Industry of Desire,* edited by Christine Gledhill. London: Routledge, 1991.

Henderson, Brian. "A Musical Comedy of Empire." In *Film Quarterly* 35, no. 2 (1981–82).

Hershfield, Joanne. *Mexican Cinema/Mexican Woman, 1940–1950.* Tucson: University of Arizona Press, 1996.

———. "Paradise Regained: Eisenstein's *Que viva México!* as Ethnography." In *Documenting the Documentary,* edited by Barry Grant and Jeannette Sloniowski. Detroit, Mich.: Wayne State University Press, 1998.

Huaco-Nuzam, Carmen. "Matilde Landeta." *Screen* 28, no. 4 (1987).

Inglis, Ruth A. *Freedom of the Movies: A Report on Self-Regulation from the Commission on Freedom of the Press.* Chicago: University of Chicago Press, 1947.

Jacobs, Lea. *The Wages of Sin: Censorship and the Fallen Woman Film, 1928–1942.* Madison: University of Wisconsin Press, 1991.

JanMohamed, Abdul R. "Sexuality on/of the Racial Border: Foucault, Wright, and the Articulation of 'Racialized Sexuality.'" In *Discourses of Sexuality: From Aristotle to AIDS,* edited by Domna C. Stanton. Ann Arbor: University of Michigan Press, 1992.

Jones, Jacquie. "The Construction of Black Sexuality." In *Black American Cinema,* edited by Manthia Diawara. New York: Routledge, 1993.

Kaplan, E. Ann. *Looking for the Other: Feminism, Film, and the Imperial Gaze.* New York: Routledge, 1997.

Keller, Gary D. *Hispanics and United States Film: An Overview and Handbook.* Tempe, Ariz.: Bilingual Press, 1994.

King, Barry. "Articulating Stardom." In *Stardom: Industry of Desire,* edited by Christine Gledhill. London: Routledge, 1991.

Kirihara, Donald. "The Accepted Idea Displaced: Stereotype and Sessue Hayakawa." In *The Birth of Whiteness: Race and the Emergence of U.S. Cinema,* edited by Daniel Bernardi. New Brunswick, N.J.: Rutgers University Press, 1996.

Kuhn, Annette. *Women's Pictures: Feminism and Cinema.* London: Verso, 1993.

Landy, Marcia. *Cinematic Uses of the Past.* Minneapolis: University of Minnesota Press, 1996.

———. *Film, Politics, and Gramsci.* Minneapolis: University of Minnesota Press, 1996.

Leff, Leonard J., and Jerold L. Simmons. *The Dame in the Kimono: Hollywood, Censorship, and the Production Code from the 1920s to the 1960s.* New York: Grove Weidenfeld, 1990.

Limerick, Patricia Nelson. *The Legacy of Conquest: The Unbroken Past of the American West.* New York: W. W. Norton, 1987.

López, Ana M. "Celluloid Tears: Melodrama in the 'Old' Mexican Cinema." *Iris* 13 (summer 1991).

———. "Are All Latins from Manhattan? Hollywood, Ethnography and Cultural Colonialism." In *Unspeakable Images: Ethnicity and the American Cinema,* edited by Lester D. Friedman. Urbana: University of Illinois Press, 1991.

Maciel, David R. "*Pochos* and Other Extremes in Mexican Cinema; or, El Cine Mexicano se va de Bracero, 1922–1963." In *Chicanos and Film: Representation and Resistance,* edited by Chon A. Noriega. Minneapolis: University of Minnesota Press, 1992.

Maltby, Richard, and Ian Craven. *Hollywood Cinema.* Oxford: Blackwell, 1995.

Marchetti, Gina. "Tragic and Transcendent Love in *The Forbidden City.*" In *The Birth of Whiteness: Race and the Emergence of U.S. Cinema,* edited by Daniel Bernardi. New Brunswick, N.J.: Rutgers University Press, 1996.

Mayne, Judith. *Private Novels, Public Films.* Athens: University of Georgia Press, 1988.

———. *Cinema and Spectatorship.* London: Routledge, 1993.

Meyer, Jean. *The Cristero Rebellion: The Mexican People between Church and State, 1926–1929.* London: Cambridge University Press, 1976.

Mitchell, Lee Clark. *Westerns: Making the Man in Fiction and Film.* Chicago: University of Chicago Press, 1994.

Monsiváis, Carlos. "De México y los chicanos, de México y su cultura fronteriza." In *La otra cara de México: El pueblo chicano,* edited by David R. Maciel. Mexico City: Ediciones "El Caballito," 1977.

———. "Mythologies." In *Mexican Cinema,* edited by Paulo Antonio Paranaguá, translated by Ana M. López. London: British Film Institute, 1995.

———. "Dolores del Río: The Face as an Institution." In *Mexican Postcards,* translated by John Kraniauskas. London: Verso, 1997.

Mulvey, Laura. "Pandora: Topographies of the Mask and Curiosity." In *Sexuality and Space,* edited by Beatriz Colomina. Princeton, N.J.: Princeton Architectural Press, 1992.

Muscio, Giuliana. *Hollywood's New Deal.* Philadelphia: Temple University Press, 1996.

Musser, Charles. "Ethnicity, Role-Playing, and American Film Comedy: From *Chinese Laundry Scene* to *Whoopee* (1894–1930)." In *Unspeakable Images: Ethnicity and the American Cinema,* edited by Lester D. Friedman. Urbana: University of Illinois Press, 1991.

Nash, Gerald D. *The Great Depression and World War II: Organizing America, 1933–1945.* New York: St. Martin's, 1979.

Niranjana, Tejaswini. *Siting Translation: History, Post-Structuralism, and the Colonial Context.* Berkeley: University of California Press, 1992.

Noriega, Chon A. "Birth of the Southwest: Social Protest, Tourism, and D. W. Griffith's *Ramona.*" In *The Birth of Whiteness: Race and the Emergence of U.S. Cinema,* edited by Daniel Bernardi. New Brunswick, N.J.: Rutgers University Press, 1996.

O'Malley, Ilene V. *The Myth of the Revolution: Hero Cults and the Institutionalization of the Mexican State, 1920–1940.* Westport, Conn.: Greenwood, 1986.

Omi, Michael, and Howard Winant. *Racial Formation in the United States: From the 1960s to the 1990s,* 2d ed. New York: Routledge, 1994.

Orellana, Margarita de. "The Circular Look: The Incursion of North American Fictional Cinema 1911-1917 into the Mexican Cinema." In *Mediating Two Worlds: Cinematic Encounters in the Americas,* edited by John King, Ana M. López, and Manuel Alvarado. London: British Film Institute, 1993.

Parrish, Michael E. *Anxious Decades: America in Prosperity and Depression, 1920–1941.* New York: W. W. Norton, 1992.

Pascoe, Peggy. "Miscegenation Law, Court Cases, and Ideologies of 'Race' in Twentieth-Century America." *Journal of American History* 83 (June 1996).

Peiss, Kathy. *Hope in a Jar: The Making of America's Beauty Culture.* New York: Henry Holt, 1998.

Pike, Frederick B. *The United States and Latin America: Myths and Stereotypes of Civilization and Nature.* Austin: University of Texas Press, 1992.

Place, J. A. *Non-Western Films of John Ford.* New York: Citadel, 1979.

Pratt, Mary Louise. "Fieldwork in Common Places." In *Writing Culture: The Poetics and Politics of Ethnography,* edited by James Clifford and George E. Marcus. Berkeley: University of California Press, 1986.

———. *Imperial Eyes: Travel Writing and Transculturation.* London: Routledge, 1992.

Ramirez Berg, Charles. "Figueroa's Skies and Oblique Perspective: Notes on the Development of the Classical Mexican Style." *Spectator* 13, no. 1 (1992): 23–38.

Ramón, David. *Historia de un rostro.* Mexico City: CCH Dirección Plantel Sur, 1993.

———. *Dolores del Río,* vols. 2 and 3. Mexico City: Clío, 1997.

Reyes, Aurelio de los. *Medio siglo de cine Mexicano (1896–1947)*. Mexico City: Editorial Trillas, 1987.

Reyes, Aurelio de los, and García Rojas, *Dolores del Río*. Mexico City: Grupo Condumex, 1996.

Ríos-Bustamante, Antonio. "Latino Participation in the Hollywood Film Industry, 1911–45." In *Chicanos and Film: Representation and Resistance*, edited by Chon A. Noriega. Minneapolis: University of Minnesota Press, 1992.

Roediger, David R. *The Wages of Whiteness: Race and the Making of the American Working Class*. New York: Verso, 1991.

Rogin, Michael P. "Kiss Me Deadly: Communism, Motherhood, and Cold War Memories." *Representations* 6 (spring 1984): 1–36.

———. "Making America Home: Racial Masquerade and Ethnic Assimilation in the Transition to Talking Pictures." *Journal of American History* 79 (December 1992).

———. *Black Face, White Noise: Jewish Immigrants in the Hollywood Melting Pot*. Berkeley: University of California Press, 1996.

Rony, Fatimah Tobing. *The Third Eye: Race, Cinema, and Ethnographic Spectacle*. Durham, N.C.: Duke University Press, 1996.

Said, Edward W. *Orientalism*. New York: Vintage, 1979.

Schatz, Thomas. *Hollywood Genres: Formulas, Filmmaking, and the Studio System*. New York: Random House, 1981.

———. "The New Hollywood." In *Film Theory Goes to the Movies*, edited by Jim Collins, Hilary Radner, and Ava Preacher Collins. New York: Routledge, 1993.

Schnitman, Jorge. *Film Industries in Latin America: Dependency and Development*. Norwood, N.J.: Ablex, 1984.

Shohat, Ella, and Robert Stam. *Unthinking Eurocentrism: Multiculturalism and the Media*. London: Routledge, 1994.

Sklar, Robert. *Movie-Made America: A Cultural History of American Movies*. New York: Random House, 1975.

Slotkin, Richard. *Gunfighter Nation: The Myth of the Frontier in Twentieth-Century America*. New York: Atheneum, 1992.

Stacey, Jackie. *Star Gazing: Hollywood Cinema and Female Spectatorship*. London: Routledge, 1994.

Staiger, Janet, *Interpreting Films: Studies in the Historical Reception of American Cinema*. Princeton, N.J.: Princeton University Press, 1992.

Stoler, Ann Laura. *Race and the Education of Desire: Foucault's History of Sexuality and the Colonial Order of Things.* Durham, N.C.: Duke University Press, 1995.

Studlar, Gaylyn. *This Mad Masquerade: Stardom and Masculinity in the Jazz Age.* New York: Columbia University Press, 1996.

Turner, Frederick Jackson. *Rereading Frederick Jackson Turner: "The Significance of the Frontier in American History" and Other Essays.* New York: Henry Holt, 1994.

Usabel, Gaizka S. de. *The High Noon of American Films in Latin America.* Ann Arbor, Mich.: UMI Research Press, 1982.

Vasey, Ruth. "Foreign Parts: Hollywood's Global Distribution and the Representation of Ethnicity." In *Movie Censorship and American Culture,* edited by Francis G. Couvares. Washington, D.C.: Smithsonian Institution Press, 1996.

———. *The World According to Hollywood, 1918–1939.* Madison: University of Wisconsin Press, 1997.

Vega Alfaro, Eduardo de la. "Origins, Development and Crisis of the Sound Cinema (1929–64)." In *Mexican Cinema,* edited by Paulo Antonio Paranaguá, translated by Ana M. López. London: British Film Institute, 1995.

Walker, Alexander. *Stardom: The Hollywood Phenomenon.* New York: Stein & Day, 1970.

Wexman, Virginia Wright. "The Family on the Land: Race and Nationhood in Silent Westerns." In *The Birth of Whiteness: Race and the Emergence of U.S. Cinema,* edited by Daniel Bernardi. New Brunswick, N.J.: Rutgers University Press, 1996.

Williams, Linda. "Film Body: An Implantation of Perversions." In *Narrative, Apparatus, Ideology,* edited by Philip Rosen. New York: Columbia University Press, 1986.

Willis, Sharon. *High Contrast: Race and Gender in Contemporary Hollywood Film.* Durham, N.C.: Duke University Press, 1997.

Wilson, Margery. *Dolores Del Rio.* Los Angeles: Chines, 1928.

Woll, Allen L. *The Latin Image in American Film.* Los Angeles: UCLA Latin American Center Publications, 1980.

Worland, Rick, and Edward Countryman. "The New Western American Historiography and the Emergence of the New American Westerns." In *Back in the Saddle Again: New Essays on the Western,* edited by Edward Buscombe and Roberta E. Pearson. London: British Film Institute, 1998.

Zinnemann, Fred. *An Autobiography: A Life in the Movies.* New York: Charles Scribner's Sons, 1992.

# Index

Joanne Hershfield is associate professor of communication studies at the University of North Carolina. She is a film and video producer and the author of *Mexican Cinema/Mexican Woman, 1940–1950*.